W9-DHF-839

POEMS

1940-1953

Also

by

Karl Shapiro:

Person, Place and Thing

V-Letter and other Poems

Essay on Rime

Trial of a Poet

POEMS

1940-1953

KARL SHAPIRO

RANDOM HOUSE

NEW YORK

 Published in New York by Random House, Inc. and simultaneously in Toronto, Canada, by Random House of Canada, Limited.

Library of Congress Catalog Card Number: 53-6928

Manufactured in the United States of America.

Designer: Ernst Reichl

Of the poems in this collection, the following appeared originally in *The New Yorker*: "A Calder," "The Bed," "Boy-Man," "Christmas Eve: Australia," "D.C.," "Homecoming," "Israel," "Love for a Hand," "The Phenomenon," "The Progress of Faust," "The Southerner," "V-Letter." Others have appeared in *A Comment, Botteghe Oscure, Chimera, Contemporary Poetry, Harper's Magazine, Meanjin, The Nation, Five Young American Poets 1941* (New Directions), *The New Republic, Partisan Review, Poetry, The Western Review.*

TO KATHY, JAKE AND LIZ

Adam and Eve 3
I THE SICKNESS OF ADAM
II THE RECOGNITION OF EVE
III THE KISS
IV THE TREE OF GUILT
V THE CONFESSION
VI SHAME
VII EXILE
Auto Wreck 13
Ballet Mécanique 15
The Bed 16
Birthday Poem 17
Blindmen 19
Boy-Man 20
Buick 22
A Calder 24
Carte Postale 25
Christmas Eve: Australia 26
The Conscientious Objector 27
Construction 28

The Contraband 29
Conscription Camp 30
A Cut Flower 32
D.C. 33
Death of Emma Goldman 34
The Dirty Word 35
The Dome of Sunday 36
Drug Store 38
Druid Hill Park 39
Ego 41
Elegy For A Dead Soldier 42
Elegy For Two Banjos 47
Elegy Written On A Frontporch 49
Emporium 52
Epitaph For John and Richard 53
The Figurehead 54
Fireworks 55
The Fly 56
F. O. Matthiessen: An Anniversary 58
Franklin 60
Full Moon: New Guinea 61
Giantess 62
Glass Poem 63
The Glutton 64
Going To School 65
Guineapig 68
The Gun 69
Haircut 70
Hill At Parramatta 71

Hollywood 72
Homecoming 74
Honkytonk 76
Hospital 78
The Intellectual 80
The Interlude 82
In The Waxworks 85
Israel 87
Israfel 88
Jefferson 89
The Leg 90
Lord, I Have Seen Too Much 91
Love For A Hand 92
Magician 93
Melbourne 95
Midnight Show 96
The Minute 98
Mongolian Idiot 99
My Grandmother 100
Necropolis 101
The New Ring 102
Nigger 103
Nostalgia 105
October 1 106
The Phenomenon 108
Piano 109
Poet 110
The Potomac 113
The Progress of Faust 114

Recapitulations 116
I
II
III
IV
V
VI
VII
VIII
Red Indian 122
A Robbery 123
Satire: Anxiety 125
Scyros 127
The Second-Best Bed 129
Six Religious Lyrics 131
The Snob 137
The Southerner 138
Sydney Bridge 140
The Synagogue 141
Terminal 143
The Tingling Back 145
To Evalyn For Christmas 147
Travelogue For Exiles 148
Troop Train 149
The Twins 151
University 152
V-Letter 154
The Voyage 156
Waitress 157
Washington Cathedral 158

POEMS

1940-1953

ADAM AND EVE

I

The Sickness of Adam

In the beginning, at every step, he turned
As if by instinct to the East to praise
The nature of things. Now every path was learned
He lost the lifted, almost flower-like gaze

Of a temple dancer. He began to walk
Slowly, like one accustomed to be alone.
He found himself lost in the field of talk;
Thinking became a garden of its own.

In it were new things: words he had never said,
Beasts he had never seen and knew were not
In the true garden, terrors, and tears shed
Under a tree by him, for some new thought.

And the first anger. Once he flung a staff
At softly coupling sheep and struck the ram.
It broke away. And God heard Adam laugh
And for his laughter made the creature lame.

And wanderlust. He stood upon the Wall
To search the unfinished countries lying wide
And waste, where not a living thing could crawl,
And yet he would descend, as if to hide.

His thought drew down the guardian at the gate,
To whom man said, 'What danger am I in?'
And the angel, hurt in spirit, seemed to hate
The wingless thing that worried after sin,

For it said nothing but marvelously unfurled
Its wings and arched them shimmering overhead,
Which must have been the signal from the world
That the first season of our life was dead.

Adam fell down with labor in his bones,
And God approached him in the cool of day
And said, 'This sickness in your skeleton
Is longing. I will remove it from your clay.'

He said also, 'I made you strike the sheep.'
It began to rain and God sat down beside
The sinking man. When he was fast asleep
He wet his right hand deep in Adam's side

And drew the graceful rib out of his breast.
Far off, the latent streams began to flow
And birds flew out of Paradise to nest
On earth. Sadly the angel watched them go.

II

The Recognition of Eve

Whatever it was she had so fiercely fought
Had fled back to the sky, but still she lay
With arms outspread, awaiting its assault,
Staring up through the branches of the tree,
The fig tree. Then she drew a shuddering breath
And turned her head instinctively his way.
She had fought birth as dying men fight death.

Her sigh awakened him. He turned and saw
A body swollen, as though formed of fruits,
White as the flesh of fishes, soft and raw.
He hoped she was another of the brutes
So he crawled over and looked into her eyes,
The human wells that pool all absolutes.
It was like looking into double skies.

And when she spoke the first word (it was *thou*)
He was terror-stricken, but she raised her hand
And touched his wound where it was fading now,
For he must feel the place to understand.
Then he recalled the longing that had torn
His side, and while he watched it whitely mend,
He felt it stab him suddenly like a thorn.

He thought the woman had hurt him. Was it she
Or the same sickness seeking to return;
Or was there any difference, the pain set free
And she who seized him now as hard as iron?
Her fingers bit his body. She looked old
And involuted, like the newly-born.
He let her hurt him till she loosed her hold.

Then she forgot him and she wearily stood
And went in search of water through the grove.

Adam could see her wandering through the wood,
Studying her footsteps as her body wove
In light and out of light. She found a pool
And there he followed shyly to observe.
She was already turning beautiful.

III

The Kiss

The first kiss was with stumbling fingertips.
Their bodies grazed each other as if by chance
And touched and untouched in a kind of dance.
Second, they found out touching with their lips.

Some obscure angel, pausing on his course,
Shed such a brightness on the face of Eve
That Adam in grief was ready to believe
He had lost her love. The third kiss was by force.

Their lips formed foreign, unimagined oaths
When speaking of the Tree of Guilt. So wide
Their mouths, they drank each other from inside.
A gland of honey burst within their throats.

But something rustling hideously overhead,
They jumped up from the fourth caress and hid.

IV

The Tree of Guilt

Why, on her way to the oracle of Love,
Did she not even glance up at the Tree
Of Life, that giant with the whitish cast
And glinting leaves and berries of dull gray,
As though covered with mold? But who would taste
The medicine of immortality,
And who would 'be as God'? And in what way?

So she came breathless to the lowlier one
And like a priestess of the cult she knelt,
Holding her breasts in token for a sign,
And prayed the spirit of the burdened bough
That the great power of the tree be seen
And lift itself out of the Tree of Guilt
Where it had hidden in the leaves till now.

Or did she know already? Had the peacock
Rattling its quills, glancing its thousand eyes
At her, the iridescence of the dove,
Stench of the he-goat, everything that joins
Told her the mystery? It was not enough,
So from the tree the snake began to rise
And dropt its head and pointed at her loins.

She fell and hid her face and still she saw
The spirit of the tree emerge and slip
Into the open sky until it stood
Straight as a standing-stone, and spilled its seed.
And all the seed were serpents of the good.
Again he seized the snake and from its lip
It spat the venomous evil of the deed.

And it was over. But the woman lay
Stricken with what she knew, ripe in her thought

Like a fresh apple fallen from the limb
And rotten, like a fruit that lies too long.
This way she rose, ripe-rotten in her prime
And spurned the cold thing coiled against her foot
And called her husband, in a kind of song.

V

The Confession

As on the first day her first word was *thou*.
He waited while she said, 'Thou art the tree.'
And while she said, almost accusingly,
Looking at nothing, 'Thou art the fruit I took.'
She seemed smaller by inches as she spoke,
And Adam wondering touched her hair and shook,
Half understanding. He answered softly, 'How?'

And for the third time, in the third way, Eve:
'The tree that rises from the middle part
Of the garden.' And almost tenderly, 'Thou art
The garden. *We*.' Then she was overcome,
And Adam coldly, lest he should succumb
To pity, standing at the edge of doom,
Comforted her like one about to leave.

She sensed departure and she stood aside
Smiling and bitter. But he asked again,
'How did you eat? With what thing did you sin?'
And Eve with body slackened and uncouth,
'Under the tree I took the fruit of truth
From an angel. I ate it with my other mouth.'
And saying so, she did not know she lied.

It was the man who suddenly released
From doubt, wept in the woman's heavy arms,
Those double serpents, subtly winding forms
That climb and drop about the manly boughs;
And dry with weeping, fiery and aroused,
Fell on her face to slake his terrible thirst
And bore her body earthward like a beast.

VI

Shame

The hard blood falls back in the manly fount,
The soft door closes under Venus' mount,
The ovoid moon moves to the Garden's side
And dawn comes, but the lovers have not died.
They have not died but they have fallen apart
In sleep, like equal halves of the same heart.

How to teach shame? How to teach nakedness
To the already naked? How to express
Nudity? How to open innocent eyes
And separate the innocent from the wise?
And how to re-establish the guilty tree
In infinite gardens of humanity?

By marring the image, by the black device
Of the goat-god, by the clown of Paradise,
By fruits of cloth and by the navel's bud,
By itching tendrils and by strings of blood,
By ugliness, by the shadow of our fear,
By ridicule, by the fig-leaf patch of hair.

Whiter than tombs, whiter than whitest clay,
Exposed beneath the whitening eye of day,
They awoke and saw the covering that reveals.
They thought they were changing into animals.
Like animals they bellowed terrible cries
And clutched each other, hiding each other's eyes.

VII

Exile

The one who gave the warning with his wings,
Still doubting them, held out the sword of flame
Against the Tree of Whiteness as they came
Angrily, slowly by, like exiled kings,

And watched them at the broken-open gate
Stare in the distance long and overlong,
And then, like peasants, pitiful and strong,
Take the first step toward earth and hesitate.

For Adam raised his head and called aloud,
'My Father, who has made the garden pall,
Giving me all things and then taking all,
Who with your opposite nature has endowed

Woman, give us your hand for our descent.
Needing us greatly, even in our disgrace,
Guide us, for gladly do we leave this place
For our own land and wished-for banishment.'

But woman prayed, 'Guide us to Paradise.'
Around them slunk the uneasy animals,
Strangely excited, uttering coughs and growls,
And bounded down into the wild abyss.

And overhead the last migrating birds,
Then empty sky. And when the two had gone
A slow half-dozen steps across the stone,
The angel came and stood among the shards

And called them, as though joyously, by name.
They turned in dark amazement and beheld
Eden ablaze with fires of red and gold,
The garden dressed for dying in cold flame,

And it was autumn, and the present world.

AUTO WRECK

Its quick soft silver bell beating, beating,
And down the dark one ruby flare
Pulsing out red light like an artery,
The ambulance at top speed floating down
Past beacons and illuminated clocks
Wings in a heavy curve, dips down,
And brakes speed, entering the crowd.
The doors leap open, emptying light;
Stretchers are laid out, the mangled lifted
And stowed into the little hospital.
Then the bell, breaking the hush, tolls once,
And the ambulance with its terrible cargo
Rocking, slightly rocking, moves away,
As the doors, an afterthought, are closed.

We are deranged, walking among the cops
Who sweep glass and are large and composed.
One is still making notes under the light.
One with a bucket douches ponds of blood
Into the street and gutter.
One hangs lanterns on the wrecks that cling,
Empty husks of locusts, to iron poles.

Our throats were tight as tourniquets,
Our feet were bound with splints, but now,
Like convalescents intimate and gauche,
We speak through sickly smiles and warn
With the stubborn saw of common sense,
The grim joke and the banal resolution.
The traffic moves around with care,
But we remain, touching a wound
That opens to our richest horror.
Already old, the question Who shall die?
Becomes unspoken Who is innocent?
For death in war is done by hands;
Suicide has cause and stillbirth, logic;
And cancer, simple as a flower, blooms.

But this invites the occult mind,
Cancels our physics with a sneer,
And spatters all we knew of denouement
Across the expedient and wicked stones.

BALLET MECANIQUE

The hand involves the wheel that weaves the hand
Without the kiss of kind; the digits flick,
The cranks obedient to no command
Raise on their iron shoulders the dead weight
For which no forges cheer. Nothing is late,
Nothing behind, excited, or too quick.
The arm involves the treadle and the wheel
Winds wakeless motion on a tireless reel.

The kiss of kind remembers wood and wool
To no cold purpose, anciently, afar:
The wheel forgets the hand that palpitates
The danceless power, and the power waits
Coiled in the tension tower for the pull
That freezes the burnt hand upon the bar.

THE BED

Your clothes of snow and satin and pure blood
Are surplices of many sacraments
Full of the woven musk of birth and death,
Full of the wet wild-flower breath of marriages,
The sweat, the slow mandragora of lust.

Meadow of sleep, table of sour sickness,
Infinite road to travel, first of graves,
Your square and subtle presence rules the house,
And little wincing hurts of everyday
Clutch at your white skirt and are comforted.

What matter if you are wise or if you know?
A third of life is yours, all that we learn
We tell you, and you dream us night by night.
We take your advice, confess in sharp detail,
Add to your knowledge, yet can teach you nothing.
"Lie here", you say, and whoever we bring you, sad,
Ashamed or delighted, you take in the spirit we give.

Let me not know too much, and let your soul
Not lead me farther on than sleep and love,
For her I marry is more white than you.
Some day, as if with ancient torches stand
And fill the walls with fires around her head,
And let your gown be fresh as April grass,
And let your prothalamium be sweet.

BIRTHDAY POEM

Five hundred nights and days ago
We kissed goodbye at the iron gates
Of the terminal, two of a crowd of twos,
Half of us mobbed away below
Where the engine pants and pants and waits,
Half of us trailing back in the snow
In taxis and cars to wait for news,
And like an enormous sign, a pair
Of blurred lips hung in the smoky air.

So far, so long, what can I say
To help commemorate your today,
What can I ever give to prove,
If proof were ever needed, love?
We are too used to words; we think
In terms of Anna, Virginia Woolf,
At times approach that dreaded brink
And stare into the selfsame gulf
That drew their splendid souls away.

We are too rich with books, our blood
Is heavy with over-thoughtful food,
Our minds are gravid—and yet to try
To backtrack to simplicity
Is fatal. Every Walden fails;
Those cynical ladies of Versailles
With silken frocks and silver pails
Playing at milkmaid sicken us.
We have our war to quicken us.

Still to be proud, still to be neat
Of smile and phrase is not for us.
The ladies of *Vogue* so vacuous,
The lips well-tailored and effete
Belong to a world that never was;
And—not to test the extremes of Swift—
The *inter faeces et urinas*

Comes to my mind, however sweet
The token of a birthday gift.

Far from the ads of gloss and glass
Of all the cities of East and West,
Today I carved with a jungle knife
An artefact of the native class,
As innocent, undemonstrative.
Blisters, sandpaper, and the best
Of scanty craftsmanship I give,
A bit of lumber cut from life,
And not to be called a primitive.

Things we step over, stones we kick
How often excel in perfect form
The treasures of miles of galleries.
I send you, darling, a polished stick
To open letters, hold in your hand.
The lovely markings smooth and warm
Grew in a palm by silent seas;
Forests of uncut trinkets stand
In groves of already perfect trees.

My trinket is more than a kiss and less,
More than a hand's twofold caress,
More than the journey it must make
Thousands of miles for remembrance' sake,
More than the world-encircling pang,
And less than the world from which it sprang,
Less than the journeying I've seen,
Less than the war of red and green,
Less than the total love I mean.

BLINDMEN

Consider them, my soul, the frightful blind!
Like mannikins, ridiculous, unbowed,
Singular, terrible, like somnambulists,
Darting their eyeballs overcast with cloud.

Their eyes from which the holy light has fled
As if far off they see, always look up;
Upon the stones of streets never look down
Inclining wearily their weighted heads . . . .

This way traverse the ever-enduring Dark,
Brother of Silence.—O Metropolis,
When all about you laugh and shout your song

With pleasure seized before this very wrong,
I cry, "I also drag myself behind!
What do they seek in Heaven, the truly blind?"

(Baudelaire translation)

BOY-MAN

England's lads are miniature men
To start with, grammar in their shiny hats,
And serious: in America who knows when
Manhood begins? Presidents dance and hug
And while the kind King waves and gravely chats
America wets on England's old green rug.

The boy-man roars. Worry alone will give
This one the verisimilitude of age.
Those white teeth are his own, for he must live
Longer, grow taller than the Texas race.
Fresh are his eyes, his darkening skin the gauge
Of bloods that freely mix beneath his face.

He knows the application of the book
But not who wrote it; shuts it like a shot.
Rather than read he thinks that he will look,
Rather than look he thinks that he will talk,
Rather than talk he thinks that he will not
Bother at all; would rather ride than walk.

His means of conversation is the joke,
Humor his language underneath which lies
The undecoded dialect of the folk.
Abroad he scorns the foreigner: what's old
Is worn, what's different bad, what's odd unwise.
He gives off heat and is enraged by cold.

Charming, becoming to the suits he wears,
The boy-man, younger than his eldest son,
Inherits the state; upon his silver hairs
Time like a panama hat sits at a tilt
And smiles. To him the world has just begun
And every city waiting to be built.

Mister, remove your shoulder from the wheel
And say this prayer, "Increase my vitamins,

Make my decisions of the finest steel,
Pour motor oil upon my troubled spawn,
Forgive the Europeans for their sins,
Establish them, that values may go on."

BUICK

As a sloop with a sweep of immaculate wing on her delicate spine
And a keel as steel as a root that holds in the sea as she leans,
Leaning and laughing, my warm-hearted beauty, you ride, you ride,
You tack on the curves with parabola speed and a kiss of goodbye,
Like a thoroughbred sloop, my new high-spirited spirit, my kiss.

As my foot suggests that you leap in the air with your hips of a girl,
My finger that praises your wheel and announces your voices of song,
Flouncing your skirts, you blueness of joy, you flirt of politeness,
You leap, you intelligence, essence of wheelness with silvery nose,
And your platinum clocks of excitement stir like the hairs of a fern.

But how alien you are from the booming belts of your birth and the smoke
Where you turned on the stinging lathes of Detroit and Lansing at night
And shrieked at the torch in your secret parts and the amorous tests,
But now with your eyes that enter the future of roads you forget;
You are all instinct with your phosphorous glow and your streaking hair.

And now when we stop it is not as the bird from the shell that I leave
Or the leathery pilot who steps from his bird with a sneer of delight,

And not as the ignorant beast do you squat and watch me
depart,
But with exquisite breathing you smile, with satisfaction of
love,
And I touch you again as you tick in the silence and settle
in sleep.

A CALDER

To raise an iron tree
Is a wooden irony,
But to cause it to sail
In a clean perpetual way
Is to play
Upon the spaces of the scale.
Climbing the stairs we say,
Is it work or is it play?

Alexander Calder made it
Work and play:
Leaves that will never burn
But were fired to be born,
Twigs that are stiff with life
And bend as to the magnet's breath,
Each segment back to back,
The whole a hanging burst of flak.

Still the base metals,
Touched by autumnal paint
Fall through no autumn
But, turning, feint
In a fall beyond trees,
Where forests are not wooded,
There is no killing breeze,
And iron is blooded.

CARTE POSTALE

It is so difficult not to go with it
Once it is seen. It tears the mind agape
With butcher force, with intellectual rape,
And the body hangs by a hair above the pit.

In whose brain, when the order was destroyed,
Did it take form and pose, and when the eye
Clicked, was he guillotined into the void
Where the vile emulsion hangs in strips to dry?

It rose with obvious relish to be viewed,
And lay at a sewer's mouth in the grainy dawn
Where a cop found it. It seemed a platitude
Like a bad postcard of the Parthenon.

I know its family tree, its dossier,
Its memory older than Pompeian walls.
Not that it lives but that it looks at day
Shocks. In the night, wherever it is, it calls,

And never fades, but lies flat and uncurled
Even in blast furnace at the fire's core,
Feeding fat tallow to our sunken world
Deep in the riches of our father's drawer.

CHRISTMAS EVE: AUSTRALIA

The wind blows hot. English and foreign birds
And insects different as their fish excite
The would-be calm. The usual flocks and herds
Parade in permanent quiet out of sight,
And there one crystal like a grain of light
Sticks in the crucible of day and cools.
A cloud burnt to a crisp at some great height
Sips at the dark condensing in deep pools.

I smoke and read my Bible and chew gum,
Thinking of Christ and Christmas of last year,
And what those quizzical soldiers standing near
Ask of the war and Christmases to come,
And sick of causes and the tremendous blame
Curse lightly and pronounce your serious name.

THE CONSCIENTIOUS OBJECTOR

The gates clanged and they walked you into jail
More tense than felons but relieved to find
The hostile world shut out, the flags that dripped
From every mother's windowpane, obscene
The bloodlust sweating from the public heart,
The dog authority slavering at your throat.
A sense of quiet, of pulling down the blind
Possessed you. Punishment you felt was clean.

The decks, the catwalks, and the narrow light
Composed a ship. This was a mutinous crew
Troubling the captains for plain decencies,
A Mayflower brim with pilgrims headed out
To establish new theocracies to west,
A Noah's ark coasting the topmost seas
Ten miles above the sodomites and fish.
These inmates loved the only living doves.

Like all men hunted from the world you made
A good community, voyaging the storm
To no safe Plymouth or green Ararat;
Trouble or calm, the men with Bibles prayed,
The gaunt politicals construed our hate.
The opposite of all armies, you were best
Opposing uniformity and yourselves;
Prison and personality were your fate.

You suffered not so physically but knew
Maltreatment, hunger, ennui of the mind.
Well might the soldier kissing the hot beach
Erupting in his face damn all your kind.
Yet you who saved neither yourselves nor us
Are equally with those who shed the blood
The heroes of our cause. Your conscience is
What we come back to in the armistice.

CONSTRUCTION

The confines of a city block
Cut to a monument, exact,
At all points rectilinear,
From air a perfect square intact,

As trim as Plato thought or Eu-
Clid drew with stick. What thinker put
This idea into cubes to sell
At fifty cents a cubic foot?

O neat, O dead, what feeling thing
Could buy so bare! O dead, O neat,
What beating heart could sink to buy
The copy of the die complete!

THE CONTRABAND

I dreamed I held a poem and knew
The capture of a living thing.
Boys in a Grecian circle sang
And women at their harvesting.

Slowly I tried to wake and draw
The vision after, word by word,
But sleep was covetous: the song
The singers and the singing blurred.

The paper flowers of everynight
All die. Day has no counterpart,
Where memory writes its boldface wish
And swiftly punishes the heart.

CONSCRIPTION CAMP

Your landscape sickens with a dry disease
Even in May, Virginia, and your sweet pines
Like Frenchmen runted in a hundred wars
Are of a child's height in these battlefields.

For Wilson sowed his teeth where generals prayed
—High-sounding Lafayette and sick-eyed Lee—
The loud Elizabethan crashed your swamps
Like elephants and the subtle Indian fell.

Is it for love, you ancient-minded towns,
That on the tidy grass of your great graves
And on your roads and riverways serene
Between the corn with green flags in a row,

Wheat amorous as hair and hills like breasts
Each generation, ignorant of the last,
Mumbling in sheds, embarrassed to salute,
Comes back to choke on etiquette of hate?

You manufacture history like jute—
Labor is cheap, Virginia, for high deeds,
But in your British dream of reputation
The black man is your conscience and your cost.

Here on the plains perfect for civil war
The clapboard city like a weak mirage
Of order rises from the sand to house
These thousands and the paranoid Monroe;

The sunrise gun rasps in the throat of heaven;
The lungs of dawn are heavy and corrupt;
We hawk and spit; our flag walks through the air
Breathing hysteria thickly in each face.

Through the long school of day, absent in heart,
Distant in every thought but self we tread,
Wheeling in blocks like large expensive toys
That never understand except through fun.

To steal aside as aimlessly as curs
Is our desire; to stare at corporals
As sceptically as boys; not to believe
The misty-eyed letter and the cheap snapshot.

To cross the unnatural frontier of your name
Is our free dream, Virginia, and beyond,
White and unpatriotic in our beds,
To rise from sleep like driftwood out of surf.

But stricter than parole is this same wall
And these green clothes, a secret on the fields,
In towns betray us to the arresting touch
Of lady-wardens, good and evil wives.

And far and fabulous is the word "Outside"
Like "Europe" when the midnight liners sailed,
Leaving a wake of ermine on the tide
Where rubies drowned and eyes were softly drunk.

Still we abhor your news and every voice
Except the Personal Enemy's, and songs
That pumped by the great central heart of love
On tides of energy at evening come.

Instinctively to break your compact law
Box within box, Virginia, and throw down
The dangerous bright habits of pure form
We struggle hideously and cry for fear.

And like a very tired whore who stands
Wrapped in the sensual crimson of her art
High in the tired doorway of a street
And beckons half-concealed the passerby,

The sun, Virginia, on your Western stairs
Pauses and smiles away between the trees,
Motioning the soldier overhill to town
To his determined hungry burst of joy.

A CUT FLOWER

I stand on slenderness all fresh and fair,
I feel root-firmness in the earth far down,
I catch in the wind and loose my scent for bees
That sack my throat for kisses and suck love.
What is the wind that brings thy body over?
Wind, I am beautiful and sick. I long
For rain that strikes and bites like cold and hurts.
Be angry, rain, for dew is kind to me
When I am cool from sleep and take my bath.

Who softens the sweet earth about my feet,
Touches my face so often and brings water?
Where does she go, taller than any sunflower
Over the grass like birds? Has she a root?
These are great animals that kneel to us,
Sent by the sun perhaps to help us grow.
I have seen death. The colors went away,
The petals grasped at nothing and curled tight.
Then the whole head fell off and left the sky.

She tended me and held me by my stalk.
Yesterday I was well, and then the gleam,
The thing sharper than frost cut me in half.
I fainted and was lifted high. I feel
Waist-deep in rain. My face is dry and drawn.
My beauty leaks into the glass like rain.
When first I opened to the sun I thought
My colors would be parched. Where are my bees?
Must I die now? Is this a part of life?

D. C.

The bad breed of the natives with their hates
That border on a Georgian night,
The short vocabulary, the southern look
That writes a volume on your past, the men
Freeholders of the city-state, the women
Polite for murder—these happen to be;
The rest arrive and never quite remain.

The rest live with an easy homelessness
And common tastelessness, their souls
Weakly lit up blazing screens and tales
Told by a newspaper. Holidays the vast
Basilicas of the railroad swallow up
Hundreds of thousands, struggling in the tide
For home, the one identity and past.

The noble riches keep themselves, the miles
Of marble breast the empty wind,
The halls of books and pictures manufacture
Their deep patinas, the fountains coldly splash
To the lone sailor, the boulevards stretch out
Farther than Arlington, where all night long
One living soldier marches for the dead.

Only the very foreign, the very proud,
The richest and the very poor
Hid in their creepy purlieus white or black
Adore this whole Augustan spectacle,
And chancelleries perceive the porch of might
Surmounted by the dome in which there lies
No Bonaparte, no Lenin, but a floor.

Yet those who govern live in quaintness, close
In the Georgian ghetto of the best;
What was the simplest of the old becomes
The exquisite palate of the new. Their names
Are admirals and paternalists, their ways
The ways of Lee who, having lost the slaves,
Died farther south, a general in the wrong.

DEATH OF EMMA GOLDMAN

Triumphant at the final breath,
Their senile God, their cops,
All the authorities and friends pro tem
Passing her pillow, keeping her concerned.
But the cowardly obit was already written:
Morning would know she was a common slut.

Russians who stood for tragedy
Were sisters all around;
Dark conscience of the family, down she lay
To end the career of passion, brain a bruise;
And mother-wonder filled her like a tide,
Rabid and raging discipline to bear.

In came the monarchist, a nurse,
And covered up her eyes;
Volkstaat of hate took over: suddenly
The Ego gagged, the Conscious overpowered,
The Memory beaten to a pulp, she fell.
It remained to hide the body, or make it laugh.

Yet not to sink her name in coin
Like Caesar was her wish,
To come alive like Frick, conjecture maps,
Or speak with kings of low mentality,
But to be left alone, a law to scorn
Of all, and none more honored than the least.

This way she died, though premature
Her clarity for others;
For it was taught that, listening, the soul
Lost track and merged with trespasses and spies
Whose black renown shook money like a rat
And showed up grass a mortmain property.

THE DIRTY WORD

The dirty word hops in the cage of the mind like the Pondicherry vulture, stomping with its heavy left claw on the sweet meat of the brain and tearing it with its vicious beak, ripping and chopping the flesh. Terrified, the small boy bears the big bird of the dirty word into the house, and grunting, puffing, carries it up the stairs to his own room in the skull. Bits of black feather cling to his clothes and his hair as he locks the staring creature in the dark closet.

All day the small boy returns to the closet to examine and feed the bird, to caress and kick the bird, that now snaps and flaps its wings savagely whenever the door is opened. How the boy trembles and delights at the sight of the white excrement of the bird! How the bird leaps and rushes against the walls of the skull, trying to escape from the zoo of the vocabulary! How wildly snaps the sweet meat of the brain in its rage.

And the bird outlives the man, being freed at the man's death-funeral by a word from the rabbi.

But I one morning went upstairs and opened the door and entered the closet and found in the cage of my mind the great bird dead. Softly I wept it and softly removed it and softly buried the body of the bird in the hollyhock garden of the house I lived in twenty years before. And out of the worn black feathers of the wing have I made pens to write these elegies, for I have outlived the bird, and I have murdered it in my early manhood.

THE DOME OF SUNDAY

With focus sharp as Flemish-painted face
In film of varnish brightly fixed
And through a polished hand-lens deeply seen,
Sunday at noon through hyaline thin air
Sees down the street,
And in the camera of my eye depicts
Row-houses and row-lives:
Glass after glass, door after door the same,
Face after face the same, the same,
The brutal visibility the same;

As if one life emerging from one house
Would pause, a single image caught between
Two facing mirrors where vision multiplies
Beyond perspective,
A silent clatter in the high-speed eye
Spinning out photo-circulars of sight.

I see slip to the curb the long machines
Out of whose warm and windowed rooms pirouette
Shellacked with silk and light
The hard legs of our women.
Our women are one woman, dressed in black.
The carmine printed mouth
And cheeks as soft as muslin-glass belong
Outright to one dark dressy man,
Merely a swagger at her curvy side.
This is their visit to themselves:
All day from porch to porch they weave
A nonsense pattern through the even glare,
Stealing in surfaces
Cold vulgar glances at themselves.

And high up in the heated room all day
I wait behind the plate glass pane for one,
Hot as a voyeur for a glimpse of one,
The vision to blot out this woman's sheen;

All day my sight records expensively
Row-houses and row-lives.

But nothing happens; no diagonal
With melting shadow falls across the curb:
Neither the blinded negress lurching through fatigue,
Nor exiles bleeding from their pores,
Nor that bright bomb slipped lightly from its rack
To splinter every silvered glass and crystal prism,
Witch-bowl and perfume bottle
And billion candle-power dressing-bulb,
No direct hit to smash the shatter-proof
And lodge at last the quivering needle
Clean in the eye of one who stands transfixed
In fascination of her brightness.

DRUG STORE

I do remember an apothecary,
And hereabouts 'a dwells

It baffles the foreigner like an idiom,
And he is right to adopt it as a form
Less serious than the living-room or bar;
　　For it disestablishes the cafe,
Is a collective, and on basic country.

Not that it praises hygiene and corrupts
The ice-cream parlor and the tobacconist's
Is it a center; but that the attractive symbols
　　Watch over puberty and leer
Like rubber bottles waiting for sick-use.

Youth comes to jingle nickels and crack wise;
The baseball scores are his, the magazines
Devoted to lust, the jazz, the Coca-Cola,
　　The lending-library of love's latest.
He is the customer; he is heroized.

And every nook and cranny of the flesh
Is spoken to by packages with wiles.
"Buy me, buy me," they whimper and cajole;
　　The hectic range of lipsticks pouts,
Revealing the wicked and the simple mouth.

With scarcely any evasion in their eye
They smoke, undress their girls, exact a stance;
But only for a moment. The clock goes round;
　　Crude fellowships are made and lost;
They slump in booths like rags, not even drunk.

DRUID HILL PARK

Be good and with me walk
The old devalued park
Where autumn has set in
The sad colors run
And a foolish East built on
The very simplest of hills
Leads us away from work
And drinks our laughter through its walls

Nor need we laugh who have
An anger fit to live
Something to build upon
That from our Conscious warm
Developed like a pun
Knows what to see and hurt
But never really raved
Being book bred to lie apart

Our Moorish no one asks
For mother's easy risks
Not here the lovers sin
To modify their ban
Some knowledge leaking in
Has rusted the roof like rain
And the whisper in the mosque
Is gone with hearts of the common run

Earth just as sweetly rots
Digesting its own fruits
Torpor adjusts to roots
And cannas set in hearts
Are lifted from their beds
O falls like winged seeds
The cry of living things
Upon whose house their death prevails

With you to apprehend
All seasons left behind

I am as child who hears
And loves what best he knows
Show me disease of bronze
Say it shall soon be gone
The poison in the wind
Removed leaving the wind alone

But for a just return
Take over hills we scorn
From years of private waste
Decades of trial and caste
Harvest our true response
To everything that grieves
To the cold light that burns
This brilliant dynasty of leaves

And give to sober sight
Now life removes his hat
Exactitude of aim
Not heavily to dream
Take all their fictions down
Like summer overthrown
Laugh in their face, show fight
Darling tell what it is to own

How lands declined like this
Abandoned piece by piece
And tax-free beautiful
Better than armies fell
O colder is just as well
We shall not hear them say
Here nature broke her lease
Here many another lover lay

EGO

Ego is not persona: in childhood
He rules the little senses, plays at eyes,
Betters the nose, learns warm and soft and cold,
Reacts but cannot act. Ego is old:
He fights but neither laughs nor cries,
Stares but is neither bad nor good.

Ego is not narcissus: if in youth
He lingers at the mirror, he is clear,
Is not in love and never seeks a friend,
Makes all dependent yet does not depend,
Inspects, indulges, does not fear,
Remembers all. Ego is truth.

Ego does not desire or acquire,
Is not the mouth and not the reaching hand,
Dreams never, sleeps at bedtime, rises first,
Sees that the hell of darkness is dispersed,
Is pale in winter, in summer tanned,
Functions alike in ice and fire.

Ego domesticated serves the man
But is no servant, stands aside for will,
Gives no advice, takes none. Ego can fail,
Pampered he softens, struck withdraws like snail.
Trust him to know and to keep still,
Love him as much as brother can.

ELEGY FOR A DEAD SOLDIER

I

A white sheet on the tail-gate of a truck
Becomes an altar; two small candlesticks
Sputter at each side of the crucifix
Laid round with flowers brighter than the blood,
Red as the red of our apocalypse,
Hibiscus that a marching man will pluck
To stick into his rifle or his hat,
And great blue morning-glories pale as lips
That shall no longer taste or kiss or swear.
The wind begins a low magnificat,
The chaplain chats, the palmtrees swirl their hair,
The columns come together through the mud.

II

We too are ashes as we watch and hear
The psalm, the sorrow, and the simple praise
Of one whose promised thoughts of other days
Were such as ours, but now wholly destroyed,
The service record of his youth wiped out,
His dream dispersed by shot, must disappear.
What can we feel but wonder at a loss
That seems to point at nothing but the doubt
Which flirts our sense of luck into the ditch?
Reader of Paul who prays beside this fosse,
Shall we believe our eyes or legends rich
With glory and rebirth beyond the void?

III

For this comrade is dead, dead in the war,
A young man out of millions yet to live,
One cut away from all that war can give,
Freedom of self and peace to wander free.
Who mourns in all this sober multitude
Who did not feel the bite of it before
The bullet found its aim? This worthy flesh,
This boy laid in a coffin and reviewed—

Who has not wrapped himself in this same flag,
Heard the light fall of dirt, his wound still fresh,
Felt his eyes closed, and heard the distant brag
Of the last volley of humanity?

IV

By chance I saw him die, stretched on the ground,
A tattooed arm lifted to take the blood
Of someone else sealed in a tin. I stood
During the last delirium that stays
The intelligence a tiny moment more,
And then the strangulation, the last sound.
The end was sudden, like a foolish play,
A stupid fool slamming a foolish door,
The absurd catastrophe, half-prearranged,
And all the decisive things still left to say.
So we disbanded, angrier and unchanged,
Sick with the utter silence of dispraise.

V

We ask for no statistics of the killed,
For nothing political impinges on
This single casualty, or all those gone,
Missing or healing, sinking or dispersed,
Hundreds of thousands counted, millions lost.
More than an accident and less than willed
Is every fall, and this one like the rest.
However others calculate the cost,
To us the final aggregate is *one,*
One with a name, one transferred to the blest;
And though another stoops and takes the gun,
We cannot add the second to the first.

VI

I would not speak for him who could not speak
Unless my fear were true: he was not wronged,
He knew to which decision he belonged

But let it choose itself. Ripe in instinct,
Neither the victim nor the volunteer,
He followed, and the leaders could not seek
Beyond the followers. Much of this he knew;
The journey was a detour that would steer
Into the Lincoln Highway of a land
Remorselessly improved, excited, new,
And that was what he wanted. He had planned
To earn and drive. He and the world had winked.

VII

No history deceived him, for he knew
Little of times and armies not his own;
He never felt that peace was but a loan,
Had never questioned the idea of gain.
Beyond the headlines once or twice he saw
The gathering of a power by the few
But could not tell their names; he cast his vote,
Distrusting all the elected but not law.
He laughed at socialism; *on mourrait*
Pour les industriels? He shed his coat
And not for brotherhood, but for his pay.
To him the red flag marked the sewer main.

VIII

Above all else he loathed the homily,
The slogan and the ad. He paid his bill
But not for Congressmen at Bunker Hill.
Ideals were few and those there were not made
For conversation. He belonged to church
But never spoke of God. The Christmas tree,
The Easter egg, baptism, he observed,
Never denied the preacher on his perch,
And would not sign Resolved That or Whereas.
Softness he had and hours and nights reserved
For thinking, dressing, dancing to the jazz.
His laugh was real, his manners were home made.

IX

Of all men poverty pursued him least;
He was ashamed of all the down and out,
Spurned the panhandler like an uneasy doubt,
And saw the unemployed as a vague mass
Incapable of hunger or revolt.
He hated other races, south or east,
And shoved them to the margin of his mind.
He could recall the justice of the Colt,
Take interest in a gang-war like a game.
His ancestry was somewhere far behind
And left him only his peculiar name.
Doors opened, and he recognized no class.

X

His children would have known a heritage,
Just or unjust, the richest in the world,
The quantum of all art and science curled
In the horn of plenty, bursting from the horn,
A people bathed in honey, Paris come,
Vienna transferred with the highest wage,
A World's Fair spread to Phoenix, Jacksonville,
Earth's capitol, the new Byzantium,
Kingdom of man—who knows? Hollow or firm,
No man can ever prophesy until
Out of our death some undiscovered germ,
Whole toleration or pure peace is born.

XI

The time to mourn is short that best becomes
The military dead. We lift and fold the flag,
Lay bare the coffin with its written tag,
And march away. Behind, four others wait
To lift the box, the heaviest of loads.
The anesthetic afternoon benumbs,
Sickens our senses, forces back our talk.
We know that others on tomorrow's roads

Will fall, ourselves perhaps, the man beside,
Over the world the threatened, all who walk:
And could we mark the grave of him who died
We would write this beneath his name and date:

EPITAPH

Underneath this wooden cross there lies
A Christian killed in battle. You who read,
Remember that this stranger died in pain;
And passing here, if you can lift your eyes
Upon a peace kept by a human creed,
Know that one soldier has not died in vain.

ELEGY FOR TWO BANJOS

Haul up the flag, you mourners,
    Not half-mast but all the way;
The funeral is done and disbanded;
    The devil's had the final say.

O mistress and wife too pensive,
    Pallbearers and priestly men,
Put your black clothes in the attic,
    And get up on your feet again.

Death did his job like a scholar,
    A most unusual case,
Death did his job like a gentleman;
    He barely disturbed the face.

You packed him in a handsome carton,
    Set the lid with silver screws;
You dug a dark pit in the graveyard
    To tell the white worms the news.

Now you've nothing left to remember,
    Nothing but the words he wrote,
But they'll never let you remember,
    Only stick like a bone in your throat.

O if I'd been his wife or mistress,
    His pallbearer or his parish priest,
I'd have kept him at home forever—
    Or as long as bric-a-brac at least.

I would have burned his body
    And salvaged a sizeable bone
For a paper-weight or a door-stop
    Or a garden flagstone.

I would have heaped the fire
    And boiled his beautiful skull.

It was laden like a ship for travels
And now is but an empty hull.

I would have dried it off in linens,
Polished it with a chamois cloth
Till it shone like a brand-new quarter
And felt smooth as the nose of a moth.

Or I'd have hung it out in the garden
Where everything else is alive,
Put a queen-bee in the brain case
So the bees could build a hive.

Maybe I'd have wired the jawbone
With a silver spring beneath,
Set it in the cradle with baby
So baby could rattle the teeth.

O you didn't do right by William
To shove him down that filthy hole,
Throw him a lot of tears and Latin
And a cheap "God bless your soul."

You might as well leave off mourning,
His photograph is getting dim,
So you'd better take a long look at it
For it's all you'll ever see of him.

Haul up the flag, you mourners,
Not half-mast but all the way;
The funeral is done and disbanded;
The devil's had the final say.

ELEGY WRITTEN ON A FRONTPORCH

The sun burns on its sultry wick;
Stratus and cumulus unite.
I who am neither well nor sick
Sit in a wicker chair and write.

A hot wind presses at my lips.
I peel. Am totally undressed.
Pinkish, as through a part-eclipse,
Heat licks upon my naked breast.

Angles in quick succession rise.
Eyesight is stereopticon
As roof and roof geometrize
Perspective deviously drawn.

I face a heaven half-destroyed,
A skyscape alabaster, dead.
One living shadow on the void,
A Flying Fortress drones ahead.

Motion and fixity take shape;
The fallow rays intensify
Distinctness. Nothing can escape
The clean hard focus of the eye.

Noise into humming noise constricts;
The traffic mumbles deeper down.
Only a trolley contradicts,
Ticks by neurotically to town.

Stretched taut upon the light I scorch,
Writhe in my sweat and smoke and sun.
The evening paper hits the porch;
My honeymoon of peace is done.

Unmasticated pulp of life . . .
Decision finds me blind and deaf.

I do not finger for the strife
Of Delano and Mutt and Jeff,

Or bend upon my nudity's
Umbilicus, the fact of facts,
As one who drowns in light and sees
The newsreel of his private acts.

I do not hug my feet with glee
And smile into my cul-de-sac
Enamoured of the dignity
Of facing forward moving back.

But set my wired sight, reclaim
The rotted friendship and the fresh;
Tune in on him who changed his name
And her who stultified the flesh.

I see who came to marriage raw
With poverty and self-abuse;
Defendants to the general law,
Their ignorance was no excuse.

Instructors, graduates I see,
Scholars who sneered into their books,
The female doctors pouring tea,
Hundreds of victims of their looks.

The money-poise of some, the pride
Of those who whored on easy checks,
Sons of The Business, dressy, snide,
Disfigured in expensive wrecks.

Believers in the songhit, thin
With pounding to the hebroid jazz;
The studious drinkers feeding in
The cloaca of the middle-class.

I see too many who romanced
Defeat, unmasculine, debased;
The striptease puritans who danced
The long lewd ritual of waste.

All these I bury out of sight
Sans benefit of epitaph.
I turn my legs into the light,
Punch out a cigarette and laugh.

For one, the best against that rout,
Deserted, obdurate to see
Their weakly literate wear out
The old Horatian fallacy;

Spoke of the beauty-to-obey,
The life-expectancy of bone.
She turned her back upon the day
But will not lie at night alone.

EMPORIUM

He must have read Aladdin who rubbed his head
And brought this out of space; some genie came
With bolts of lawn and rugs of heavy red,
Shoes for white boxes, gems for velvet trays;
For who could authorize in his right name
Such pricelessness of time and recklessness of days?

Not Faust, who longed for Hell, would sell his light
For moving stairs and mirrors set in miles
Where wives might wander with their sex in sight;
Rage and rat's-logic this man must have known
Who built these buttresses on rotted piles,
Initialed every brick, and carved his lips in stone.

As if the ancient principle obtained
And solvent time would underwrite his debt,
Or the strong face of flesh were not profaned
For mannikins with hair of cloth-of-gold;
As if no tongue had ever questioned yet
Who buys and who is bought, who sells and who is sold.

But those politely dressed in normal drab
Shall think of him remotely, think with shame
How of their skill, their goodness and their gab
He trained his joys to be obsequious Jews;
At last not even wives shall goad his name
To feats of wealth, humility, and sickness-news;

So that, with rounded ruins honored, like Stonehenge,
Time shall have time, and he his impotent revenge.

EPITAPH FOR JOHN AND RICHARD

There goes the clock; there goes the sun;
Greenwich is right with Arlington;
The signal's minutes are signifying
That somebody old has finished dying,
That somebody young has just begun.

What do you think you earned today
Except the waste, except the pay,
Except the power to be spending?
And now your year is striking, ending,
What do you think you have put away?

Only a promise, only a life
Squandered in secret with a wife
In bedtime feigning and unfeigning;
The blood has long since ceased complaining;
The clock has satisfied the strife.

They will not cast your honored head
Or say from lecterns what you said,
But only keep you with them all
Committed in the City Hall;
Once born, once married, and once dead.

THE FIGUREHEAD

Watching my paralytic friend
Caught in the giant clam of himself
Fast on the treacherous shoals of his bed,
I look away to the place he had left
Where at a decade's distance he appeared
To pause in his walk and think of a limp.
One day he arrived at the street bearing
The news that he dragged an ancient foot:
The people on their porches seemed to sway.

Though there are many wired together
In this world and the next, my friend
Strains in his clamps. He is all sprung
And locked in the rust of inner change.
The therapist who plucks him like a harp
Is a cold torture: the animal bleats
And whimpers on its far seashore
As she leans to her find with a smooth hunger.

Somewhere in a storm my pity went down:
It was a wooden figurehead
With sea-hard breasts and polished mouth.
But women wash my friend with brine
From shallow inlets of their eyes,
And women rock my friend with waves
That pulsate from the female moon.
They gather at his very edge and haul
My driftwood friend toward their fires.

Speaking of dancing, joking of sex,
I watch my paralytic friend
And seek my pity in those wastes where he
Becomes my bobbing figurehead.
Then as I take my leave I wade
Loudly into the shallows of his pain,
I splash like a vacationer,
I scare his legs and stir the time of day
With rosy clouds of sediment.

FIREWORKS

In midsummer darkness when primeval silences close
On the women in linen and children and husbands in
blouses
We gather in laughter and move with a current that flows
Through the intimate suburbs of ice-cream and talkative
houses

To a fabulous field of the night of the rainbows of ages
Where blindness is dyed with the blooms and the tints of
desire,
And the wars of our boyhood rise up from the oldest of pages
With heroes erected on billboards of fuses and wire.

In the garden of pleistocene flowers we wander like Alice
Where seed sends a stalk in the heavens and pops from a
pod
A blue blossom that hangs on the distance and opens its
chalice
And falls in the dust of itself and goes out with a nod.

How the hairy tarantulas crawl in the soft of the ether
Where showers of lilies explode in the jungle of creepers;
How the rockets of sperm hurtle up to the moon and beneath
her
Deploy for the eggs of the astral and sorrowful sleepers!

And the noble bombardment that bursts in the depth of our
ears
Lifts the hair of our heads and interprets in absolute noises
The brimstone of total destruction, the doom of our years.
O the Judgement that shatters the rose of our secrets and
poises!

In Niagaras of fire we leak in the luminous aura
And gasp at the portrait of Lincoln alive on the lattice.
Our history hisses and spits in the burning Gomorrah,
The volcanoes subside; we are given our liberty gratis.

THE FLY

O hideous little bat, the size of snot,
With polyhedral eye and shabby clothes,
To populate the stinking cat you walk
The promontory of the dead man's nose,
Climb with the fine leg of a Duncan-Phyfe
  The smoking mountains of my food
    And in a comic mood
  In mid-air take to bed a wife.

Riding and riding with your filth of hair
On gluey foot or wing, forever coy,
Hot from the compost and green sweet decay,
Sounding your buzzer like an urchin toy—
You dot all whiteness with diminutive stool,
  In the tight belly of the dead
    Burrow with hungry head
  And inlay maggots like a jewel.

At your approach the great horse stomps and paws
Bringing the hurricane of his heavy tail;
Shod in disease you dare to kiss my hand
Which sweeps against you like an angry flail;
Still you return, return, trusting your wing
  To draw you from the hunter's reach
    That learns to kill to teach
  Disorder to the tinier thing.

My peace is your disaster. For your death
Children like spiders cup their pretty hands
And wives resort to chemistry of war.
In fens of sticky paper and quicksands
You glue yourself to death. Where you are stuck
  You struggle hideously and beg
    You amputate your leg
  Imbedded in the amber muck.

But I, a man, must swat you with my hate,
Slap you across the air and crush your flight,

Must mangle with my shoe and smear your blood,
Expose your little guts pasty and white,
Knock your head sidewise like a drunkard's hat,
  Pin your wings under like a crow's,
    Tear off your flimsy clothes
  And beat you as one beats a rat.

Then like Gargantua I stride among
The corpses strewn like raisins in the dust,
The broken bodies of the narrow dead
That catch the throat with fingers of disgust.
I sweep. One gyrates like a top and falls
  And stunned, stone blind, and deaf
    Buzzes its frightful F
  And dies between three cannibals.

F. O. MATTHIESSEN: AN ANNIVERSARY

To learn the meaning of his leap to death
What need to know the wounds he carried down
To his crushing sleep? For the shocked town,
Bombed by his suicide, the ejaculation of blood,
Summarized it neatly in the shibboleth
Of mutual forgiveness: Matthiessen was good.

Yet there remained a reminder on the stair
Of nothing: high on the ledge of that hotel
Where an unbalanced soldier heard the yell
Of the depraved unchristian mob to leap,
But could not, being imperfect in despair,
Jump at their will into a hell so deep,

And fell back finally in the waiting arms
Of a traffic cop, a blond girl, and a priest.
And thus the loud and thousand-handed beast
Melted away. — What mob did Matthiessen
Hear chanting in rhythm, and what uniforms
Tried to retrieve him to the world of men?

What was he saying in his heavy fall
Through space, so broken by the hand of stone?
What word was that stopped like a telephone
Torn with its nervous wire from the wall?
Does not the condemned man raise his voice to call
His phrase of justice down the empty hall?

And who betrayed him finally. Was it I?
Some poet who turned his praises into blame,
Or some historian of the parlor game
Of war? Or the easy capture of the schloss
By Slavs? The Americanization of the spy?
The death of a friend? Was there no further loss?

Left with no ground except the ground that kills,
He mourned the death of politics and died.

It was, as it were, a statesman's suicide,
For when out of the window he had flung
His life upon those uncharitable hills,
Did he not will his charity to the young?

FRANKLIN

The star of Reason, Ben, reposed in you
Octagon spectacles, a sparking kite,
Triggers and jiggers, bobbins, reels and screws,
And aphorisms spelled in black and white.

Wiseacre, editor, and diplomat,
First of the salesmen, hero of the clerk,
The logic of invention led to bells
Joyous for George and terrible for Burke.

Poor Richard prospers and the grocery man
Has your disarming prose and pays his tax.
Sir, what is the reason for this bird
That sings and screams and coos and crows and quacks?

Two-penny buns, a whistle for the boy,
Rare Ben, the printer's devil used you well.
Lenin and Freud embroider left and right
And Curtis beats The Independence Bell.

FULL MOON: NEW GUINEA

These nights we fear the aspects of the moon,
Sleep lightly in the radiance falling clear
On palms and ferns and hills and us; for soon
The small burr of the bombers in our ear
Tickles our rest; we rise as from a nap
And take our helmets absently and meet,
Prepared for any spectacle or mishap,
At trenches fresh and narrow at our feet.

Look up, look up, and wait and breathe. These nights
We fear Orion and the Cross. The crowd
Of deadly insects caught in our long lights
Glitter and seek to burrow in a cloud
Soft-mined with high explosive. Breathe and wait,
The bombs are falling darkly for our fate.

GIANTESS

When Nature once in lustful hot undress
Conceived gargantuan offspring, then would I
Have loved to live near a young giantess,
Like a voluptuous cat at a queen's feet.

To see her body flower with her desire
And freely spread out in its dreadful play,
Guess if her heart concealed some heavy fire
Whose humid smokes would swim upon her eye;

To feel at leisure her stupendous shapes,
Crawl on the cliffs of her enormous knees,
And, when the unhealthy summer suns fatigued,

Have her stretch out across the plains and so
Sleep in the shadows of her breasts at ease
Like a small hamlet at a mountain's base.

(Baudelaire translation)

GLASS POEM

The afternoon lies glazed upon the wall
And on the window shines the scene-like bay,
And on the dark reflective floor a ray
Falls, and my thoughts like ashes softly fall.

And I look up as one who looks through glass
And sees the thing his soul clearly desires,
Who stares until his vision flags and tires,
But from whose eye the image fails to pass;

Until a wish crashes the vitreous air
And comes to your real hands across this space,
Thief-like and deeply cut to touch your face,
Dearly, most bitterly to touch your hair.

And I could shatter these transparent lights,
Could thrust my arms and bring your body through,
Break from the subtle spectrum the last hue
And change my eyes to dark soft-seeing nights.

But the sun stands and the hours stare like brass
And day flows thickly into permanent time,
And toward your eyes my threatening wishes climb
Where you move through a sea of solid glass.

THE GLUTTON

The jowls of his belly crawl and swell like the sea
When his mandibles oily with lust champ and go wide;
Eternal, the springs of his spittle leak at the lips
Suspending the tongue like a whale that rolls on the tide.

His hands are as rotten fruit. His teeth are as corn.
Deep are the wells of his eyes and like navels, blind.
Dough is the brain that supplies his passion with bread.
Dough is the loose-slung sack of his great behind.

Will his paps become woman's? He dreams of the yielding
    of milk,
Despising the waste of his stool that recalls him to bread;
More than passion of sex and the transverse pains of disease
He thinks of starvation, the locked-up mouth of the dead.

I am glad that his stomach will eat him away in revenge,
Digesting itself when his blubber is lain in the earth.
Let the juice of his gluttony swallow him inward like lime
And leave of his volume only the mould of his girth.

GOING TO SCHOOL

What shall I teach in the vivid afternoon
With the sun warming the blackboard and a slip
Of cloud catching my eye?
Only the cones and sections of the moon
Out of some flaking page of scholarship,
Only some foolish heresy
To counteract the authority of prose.
The ink runs freely and the dry chalk flows
Into the silent night of seven slates
Where I create the universe as if
It grew out of some old rabbinic glyph
Or hung upon the necessity of Yeats.

O dry imaginations, drink this dust
That grays the room and powders my coat sleeve,
For in this shaft of light
I dance upon the intellectual crust
Of our own age and hold this make-believe
Like holy-work before your sight.
This is the list of books that time has burned,
These are the lines that only poets have learned,
The frame of dreams, the symbols that dilate;
Yet when I turn from this dark exercise
I meet your bright and world-considering eyes
That build and build and never can create.

I gaze down on the garden with its green
Axial lines and scientific pond
And watch a man in white
Stiffly pursue a butterfly between
Square hedges where he takes it overhand
Into the pocket of his net.
Ah psyche, sinking in the bottled fumes,
Dragging your slow wings while the hunt resumes.
I say, "He placed an image on the pool
Of the Great Mind to float there like a leaf
And then sink downward to the dark belief
Of the Great Memory of the Hermetic School."

I say, "Linnaeus drowned the names of flowers
With the black garlands of his Latin words;
The gardens now are his,
The drug-bright blossoms of the glass are ours.
I think a million taxidermist's birds
Sing in the mind of Agassiz
Who still retained one image of the good,
Who said a fish is but a thought of God.
—This is the flat world circled by its dogs,
This is the right triangle held divine
Before bald Euclid drew his empty line
And shame fell on the ancient astrologues."

The eyes strike angles on the farther wall,
Divine geometry forms upon the page,
I feel a sense of shame.
Then as the great design begins to pall
A cock crows in a laboratory cage
And I proceed. "As for the name,
It is the potency itself of thing,
It is the power-of-rising of the wing;
Without it death and feathers, for neither reed
Of Solomon nor quill of Shakespeare's goose
Ever did more or less than to deduce
Letter from number in our ignorant creed."

And what if he who blessed these walls should walk
Invisibly in the room? — My conscience prates,
"The great biologist
Who read the universe in a piece of chalk
Said all knowledge is good, all learning waits,
And wrong hypotheses exist
To order knowledge and to set it right.
We burn, he said, that others may have light.
These are the penetralia of the school
Of the last century. Under a later sky
We call both saint and fool to prophesy
The second cycle brimming at the full."

Then the clock strikes and I erase the board,
Clearing the cosmos with a sweep of felt,
Voiding my mind as well.
Now that the blank of reason is restored
And they go talking of the crazy Celt
And ghosts that sipped his muscatel,
I must escape their laughter unaware
And sidle past the question on the stair
To gain my office. Is the image lost
That burned and shivered in the speculum
Or does it hover in the upper room?
Have I deceived the student or the ghost?

Here in the quiet of the book-built dark
Where masonry of volumes walls me in
I should expect to find,
Returning to me on a lower arc,
Some image bodying itself a skin,
Some object thinking forth a mind.
This search necessitates no closer look.
I close my desk and choose a modern book
And leave the building. Low, as to astound,
The sun stands with its body on the line
That separates us. Low, as to combine,
The sun touches its image to the ground.

GUINEAPIG

What do you care, dear total stranger,
For the successful failure of my safest danger,
My pig in the poke or dog in the manger,

Or who does what in the where of his chamber
Probing for his gallstones and the rods of amber
When the succubae sing and the accusers clamber?

Tooth for a Tooth, O why will you wander
After somebody's anybody's body to squander?
Do the heads grow bald as the hands grow fonder?

Thank you. Your kiss of conditional surrender
Reminds me of the case of dubious gender
Who died on the verge of gaining a defender.

Then read it and weep, dear lovelorn panther;
Change your pajamas and fill the decanter;
Down with the dreamwork and long live the banter.

THE GUN

You were angry and manly to shatter the sleep of your
throat;
The kiss of your blast is upon me, O friend of my fear,
And I savour your breath like a perfume as salt and austere
As the scent of the thunder of heaven that brims in the
moat!

I grip you. We lie on the ground in the thongs of our clasp
And we stare like the hunter who starts at a tenuous cry;
We have wounded the wind with a wire and stung in the
sky
A white hole that is small and unseen as the bite of the asp.

The smooth of your cheek—Do you sight from the depth of
your eye
More faultless than vision, more true than the aiming of
stars?
Is the heart of your hatred the target of redness of Mars
Or the roundness of heart of the one who must stumble and
die?

O the valley is silent and shocked. I absolve from your name
The exaction of murder, my gun. It is I who have killed.
It is I whose enjoyment of horror is fine and fulfilled.
You are only the toy of my terror, my emblem of blame.

Come with me. We shall creep for his eyes like the sweat of
my skin,
For the wind is repaired and the fallen is calling for breath.
You are only the means of the practical humor of death
Which is savage to punish the dead for the sake of my sin!

HAIRCUT

O wonderful nonsense of lotions of Lucky Tiger,
Of savory soaps and oils of bottle-bright green,
The gold of liqueurs, the unguents of Newark and Niger,
Powders and balms and waters washing me clean;

In mirrors of marble and silver I see us forever
Increasing, decreasing the puzzles of luminous spaces
As I turn, am revolved and am pumped in the air on a lever,
With the backs of my heads in chorus with all of my faces.

Scissors and comb are mowing my hair into neatness,
Now pruning my ears, now smoothing my neck like a plain;
In the harvest of hair and the chaff of powdery sweetness
My snow-covered slopes grow dark with the wooly rain.

And the little boy cries, for it hurts to sever the curl,
And we too are quietly bleating to part with our coat.
Does the barber want blood in a dish? I am weak as a girl,
I desire my pendants, the fatherly chin of a goat.

I desire the pants of a bear, the nap of a monkey
Which trousers of friction have blighted down to my skin.
I am bare as a tusk, as jacketed up as a flunkey,
With the chest of a moth-eaten camel growing within.

But in death we shall flourish, you summer-dark leaves of
    my head,
While the flesh of the jaw ebbs away from the shores of my
    teeth;
You shall cover my sockets and soften the boards of my bed
And lie on the flat of my temples as proud as a wreath.

HILL AT PARRAMATTA

Just like a wave, the long green hill of my desire
Rides to the shore-like level here to engulf us all
Who work and joke in the hollow grave and the shallow
mire
Where we must dig or else the earth will truly fall.

Long as a comber, green as grass, taut as a tent,
And there far out like specks the browsing cattle drift,
And sweet sweet with the green of life and the downhill
scent,
O sweet at the heart such heavy loveliness to lift!

And you know best the void of the world, the blue and
green,
And the races departing single file to the west to die—
But all your memory shines on the tiny deaths you have
seen
No more nor less than the point of light in the tear of my
eye:

So proud of the wave, my womanly hill, to lean on the shore
And tumble the sands and flatness of death with your silent
roar.

HOLLYWOOD

Farthest from any war, unique in time
Like Athens or Baghdad, this city lies
Between dry purple mountains and the sea.
The air is clear and famous, every day
Bright as a postcard, bringing bungalows
   And sights. The broad nights advertise
For love and music and astronomy.

Heart of a continent, the hearts converge
On open boulevards where palms are nursed
With flare-pots like a grove, on villa roads
Where castles cultivated like a style
Breed fabulous metaphors in foreign stone,
   And on enormous movie lots
Where history repeats its vivid blunders.

Alice and Cinderella are most real.
Here may the tourist, quite sincere at last,
Rest from his dream of travels. All is new,
No ruins claim his awe, and permanence,
Despised like customs, fails at every turn.
   Here where the eccentric thrives,
Laughter and love are leading industries.

Luck is another. Here the bodyguard,
The parasite, the scholar are well paid,
The quack erects his alabaster office,
The moron and the genius are enshrined,
And the mystic makes a fortune quietly;
   Here all superlatives come true
And beauty is marketed like a basic food.

O can we understand it? Is it ours,
A crude whim of a beginning people,
A private orgy in a secluded spot?
Or alien like the word *harem*, or true

Like hideous Pittsburgh or depraved Atlanta?
  Is adolescence just as vile
As this its architecture and its talk?

Or are they parvenus, like boys and girls?
Or ours and happy, cleverest of all?
Yes. Yes. Though glamorous to the ignorant
This is the simplest city, a new school.
What is more nearly ours? If soul can mean
  The civilization of the brain,
This is a soul, a possible proud Florence.

HOMECOMING

Lost in the vastness of the void Pacific
My thousand days of exile, pain,
Bid me farewell. Gone is the Southern Cross
To her own sky, fallen a continent
Under the wave, dissolved the bitterest isles
In their salt element,
And here upon the deck the mist encloses
My smile that would light up all darkness
And ask forgiveness of the things that thrust
Shame and all death on millions and on me.

We bring no raw materials from the East
But green-skinned men in blue-lit holds
And lunatics impounded between-decks;
The mighty ghoul-ship that we ride exhales
The sickly-sweet stench of humiliation,
And even the majority, untouched by steel
Or psychoneurosis, stare with eyes in rut,
Their hands a rabble to snatch the riches
Of glittering shops and girls.

Because I am angry at this kindness which
Is both habitual and contradictory
To the life of armies, now I stand alone
And hate the swarms of khaki men that crawl
Like lice upon the wrinkled hide of earth,
Infesting ships as well. Not otherwise
Could I lean outward piercing fog to find
Our sacred bridge of exile and return.
My tears are psychological, not poems
To the United States; my smile is prayer.

Gnawing the thin slops of anxiety,
Escorted by the ground swell and by gulls,
In silence and with mystery we enter
The territorial waters. Not till then
Does that convulsive terrible joy, more sudden

And brilliant than the explosion of a ship,
Shatter the tensions of the heaven and sea
To crush a hundred thousand skulls
And liberate in that high burst of love
The imprisoned souls of soldiers and of me.

HONKYTONK

Taken as diagram of Mind that marks,
Led by an arrow, green perimeters
Where thoughts sip peace and garden; inward then
To suffering junctions, slums kicked by a boot,
        Arpeggios of porches:
        Decision, Anger, Pride,
Like Self-Reproach the city points to this
Its maudlin slapping heart, our origin.

Then at the outskirts of our Conscious, No
From old high-over offices beats down
On standard faces Business-mad, and girls,
Grass under sullen stone, grown pale with work;
        Yet shields with shadow this
        Disgraced like genitals
Ghetto of local sin, laughable Hell,
Night's very alley, loathed but let alone.

I say to harass projects of decorum
This is maintained by kids, police, douceurs,
And ravenous for marvels, rancid Jews.
Callow as brass, their eyes on nipples snagged,
        Snagged in the jaded hair,
        Goaded by silken legs,
They mill around, bacterial and bright,
Seeking outbreaks of pain, their bitter milk.

Who needs Revenge or Fear can buy: in bars
Murals of lust, and talk; movies for men;
A waxworks of syphilitics; shooting range,
Phrenologist and tattoo artist; all
        Quacks who apprehend
        And speak the dirty word.
But oh, ridiculously lost those four
Hymning salvation at the Burlesk door.

How elemental ions of pure joy
Convert to deadly sins, and bump like trucks

Uptown to roads instinctive to the young,
I only ask. But in and out they go
Satanic to discover
Imago of Unrest
Whose Ultima Thule is a general low
And obscene civics of our self-distrust.

HOSPITAL

Inside or out, the key is pain. It holds
The florist to your pink medicinal rose,
The nickname to the corpse. One wipes it from
Blue German blades or drops it down the drain;
The novelist with a red tube up his nose
Gingerly pets it. Nurse can turn it off.

This is the Oxford of all sicknesses.
Kings have lain here and fabulous small Jews
And actresses whose legs were always news.
In this black room the painter lost his sight,
The crippled dancer here put down her shoes,
And the scholar's memory broke, like an old clock.

These reached to heaven and inclined their heads
While starchy angels reached them into beds:
These stooped to hell to labor out their time,
Or choked to death in seas of glaucous slime:
All tasted fire, and then, their hate annealed,
Ate sad ice-cream and wept upon a child.

What church is this, what factory of souls
Makes the bad good and fashions a new nose,
And the doctors reel with Latin and even the dead
Expect the unexpected? For O the souls
Fly back like heavy homing-birds to roost
In long-racked limbs, filling the lonely boughs.

The dead cry *life* and stagger up the hill;
But is there still the incorrigible city where
The well enjoy their poverty and the young
Worship the gutter? Is Wednesday still alive
And Tuesday wanting terribly to sin?
Hush, there are many pressing the oak doors,

Saying, "Are boys and girls important fears?
Can you predict the elections by my guts?"

But the rubber gloves are deep in a deep wound,
Stitching a single heart. These far surpass
Themselves, their wives, and the removed goitre;
Are, for the most part, human but unbandaged.

THE INTELLECTUAL

What should the wars do with these jigging fools?

The man behind the book may not be man,
His own man or the book's or yet the time's,
But still be whole, deciding what he can
In praise of politics or German rimes;

But the intellectual lights a cigarette
And offers it lit to the lady, whose odd smile
Is the merest hyphen—lest he should forget
What he has been resuming all the while.

He talks to overhear, she to withdraw
To some interior feminine fireside
Where the back arches, beauty puts forth a paw
Like a black puma stretching in velvet pride,

Making him think of cats, a stray of which
Some days sets up a howling in his brain,
Pure interference such as this neat bitch
Seems to create from listening disdain.

But talk is all the value, the release,
Talk is the very fillip of an act,
The frame and subject of the masterpiece
Under whose film of age the face is cracked.

His own forehead glows like expensive wood,
But back of it the mind is disengaged,
Self-sealing clock recording bad and good
At constant temperature, intact, unaged.

But strange, his body is an open house
Inviting every passerby to stay;
The city to and fro beneath his brows
Wanders and drinks and chats from night to day.

Think of a private thought, indecent room
Where one might kiss his daughter before bed!
Life is embarrassed; shut the family tomb,
Console your neighbor for his recent dead;

Do something! die in Spain or paint a green
Gouache, go into business (Rimbaud did),
Or start another Little Magazine,
Or move in with a woman, have a kid.

Invulnerable, impossible, immune,
Do what you will, your will will not be done
But dissipate the light of afternoon
Till evening flickers like the midnight sun,

And midnight shouts and dies: I'd rather be
A milkman walking in his sleep at dawn
Bearing fat quarts of cream, and so be free,
Crossing alone and cold from lawn to lawn.

I'd rather be a barber and cut hair
Than walk with you in gilt museum halls,
You and the puma-lady, she so rare
Exhaling her silk soul upon the walls.

Go take yourselves apart, but let me be
The fault you find with everyman. I spit,
I laugh, I fight; and you, *l'homme qui rît*,
Swallow your stale saliva, and still sit.

THE INTERLUDE

I

Much of transfiguration that we hear,
The ballet of the atoms, the second law
Of thermo-dynamics, Isis, and the queer

Fertilization of fish, the Catholic's awe
For the life-cycle of the Nazarene,
His wife whom sleeping Milton thought he saw;

Much of the resurrection that we've seen
And taken part in, like the Passion Play,
All of autumnal red and April green,

To those who walk in work from day to day,
To economic and responsible man,
All, all is substance. Life that lets him stay

Uses his substance kindly while she can
But drops him lifeless after his one span.

II

What lives? the proper creatures in their homes?
A weed? the white and giddy butterfly?
Bacteria? necklaces of chromosomes?

What lives? the breathing bell of the clear sky?
The crazed bull of the sea? Andean crags?
Armies that plunge into themselves to die?

People? A sacred relic wrapped in rags,
The ham-bone of a saint, the winter rose,
Do these?—And is there not a hand that drags

The bottom of the universe for those
Who still perhaps are breathing? Listen well,
There lives a quiet like a cathedral close

At the soul's center where substance cannot dwell
And life flowers like music from a bell.

III

Writing, I crushed an insect with my nail
And thought nothing at all. A bit of wing
Caught my eye then, a gossamer so frail

And exquisite, I saw in it a thing
That scorned the grossness of the thing I wrote.
It hung upon my finger like a sting.

A leg I noticed next, fine as a mote,
"And on this frail eyelash he walked," I said,
"And climbed and walked like any mountain-goat."

And in this mood I sought the little head,
But it was lost; then in my heart a fear
Cried out, "A life—why beautiful, why dead!"

It was a mite that held itself most dear,
So small I could have drowned it with a tear.

IN THE WAXWORKS

At midday when the light rebukes the world,
Searching the seams of faces, cracks of walls
And each fault of the beautiful,
Seized by a panic of the street I fled
Into a waxworks where the elite in crime
And great in fame march past in fixed parade.
How pale they were beneath their paint, how pure
The monsters gleaming from the cubicles!

When, as in torsion, I beheld
These malformations of the evil mind
I grew serene and seemed to fall in love,
As one retiring to a moving picture
Or to a gallery of art. I saw
The basest plasm of the human soul
Here turned to sculpture, fingering,
Kissing, and corrupting life.

So back and forth among the leers of wax
I strutted for the idols of the tribe,
Aware that I was on display, not they,
And that I had come down to pray,
As one retires to a synagogue
Or to a plaster saint upon the wall.
Why were these effigies more dear to me
Than haughty mannikins in a window-shop?

I said a rosary for the Presidents
And fell upon my knees before
The Ripper and an exhibit of disease
Revolting more in its soft medium
Than in the flesh. I stroked a prince's hand,
Leaving a thumbprint in the palm. I swore
Allegiance to the suicide whose wrists
Of tallow bled with admirable red.

Why were these images more dear to me
Than faïence dolls or gods of smooth Pentelikon?

Because all statuary turns to death
And only half-art balances.
The fetish lives, idolatry is true,
The crude conception of the putrid face
Sticks to my heart. This criminal in wan
Weak cerement of translucent fat

Is my sweet saint. O heretic, O mute,
When broils efface the Metropolitan
And swinish man from some cloaca creeps
Or that deep midden, his security,
Coming to you in brutish admiration
May he look soft into your eyes;
And you, good wax, may you not then despise
Our sons and daughters, fallen apes.

ISRAEL

When I think of the liberation of Palestine,
When my eye conceives the great black English line
Spanning the world news of two thousand years,
My heart leaps forward like a hungry dog,
My heart is thrown back on its tangled chain,
My soul is hangdog in a Western chair.

When I think of the battle for Zion I hear
The drop of chains, the starting forth of feet
And I remain chained in a Western chair.
My blood beats like a bird against a wall,
I feel the weight of prisons in my skull
Falling away; my forebears stare through stone.

When I see the name of Israel high in print
The fences crumble in my flesh; I sink
Deep in a Western chair and rest my soul.
I look the stranger clear to the blue depths
Of his unclouded eye. I say my name
Aloud for the first time unconsciously.

Speak of the tillage of a million heads
No more. Speak of the evil myth no more
Of one who harried Jesus on his way
Saying, *Go faster*. Speak no more
Of the yellow badge, *secta nefaria*.
Speak the name only of the living land.

ISRAFEL

la tombe de Poe éblouissante

Picture the grave in his diabolical dream
Where death would come with clues and scenery,
The bulbous forehead and the crooked mouth
Leaking a poison, the translucent hands.

Perhaps like Juliet he could come alive
To hate Longfellow and to outrage life,
But dare not from his wretched rusty stone,
Landmark for girls developing in slums.

Here he is local color, another crank;
Pawnshops and whores and sour little bars
Accept him. Neither alarming nor prophetic,
He pleases like a wop or a jack-o-lantern.

Others uptown forgive his nasty eyes
Because he was sick and had a mind to err;
But he was never dirty like Hawthorne,
But boyish with his spooks and funerals

And clammy virgins. What else were his codes
But diagrams of hideouts of the mind
Plugged up with corpses and expensive junk,
Prosopopoeia to keep himself at bay?

Think of him as a cicerone with data
False as a waxworks and that understood
Ask pitifully for pain. Or think that now
Four cities claim him as France recommended.

JEFFERSON

If vision can dilate, my noble lord,
Farther than porticos, Italian cells,
Newtonian gardens, Haydn, and cuisine,
Tell us, most serious of all our poets,
Why is the clock so low?

I see the tender gradient of your will;
Virginia is the Florence of your soul,
Yes, ours. The architecture of your hands
Quiets ambition and revives our skill
And buys our faithlessness.

So temperate, so remote, so sure of phrase,
Your music sweeps a continent, a sphere,
Fashions a modern language for a war
And by its cadence makes responsible
Our million names to you.

When you were old the god of government
Seemed to recede a pace, and you were glad.
You watched the masons through your telescope
Finish your school of freedom. Death itself
Stood thoughtful at your bed.

And now the surfaces of mind are rubbed
Our essence starts like serum from our eyes.
How can you not assume the deities
That move behind the bloodshot look and lean
Like saints and Salem devils?

THE LEG

Among the iodoform, in twilight-sleep,
What have I lost? he first inquires,
Peers in the middle distance where a pain,
Ghost of a nurse, hazily moves, and day,
Her blinding presence pressing in his eyes
And now his ears. They are handling him
With rubber hands. He wants to get up.

One day beside some flowers near his nose
He will be thinking, *When will I look at it*?
And pain, still in the middle distance, will reply,
At what? and he will know it's gone,
O where! and begin to tremble and cry.
He will begin to cry as a child cries
Whose puppy is mangled under a screaming wheel.

Later, as if deliberately, his fingers
Begin to explore the stump. He learns a shape
That is comfortable and tucked in like a sock.
This has a sense of humor, this can despise
The finest surgical limb, the dignity of limping,
The nonsense of wheel-chairs. Now he smiles to the wall:
The amputation becomes an acquisition.

For the leg is wondering where he is (all is not lost)
And surely he has a duty to the leg;
He is its injury, the leg is his orphan,
He must cultivate the mind of the leg,
Pray for the part that is missing, pray for peace
In the image of man, pray, pray for its safety,
And after a little it will die quietly.

The body, what is it, Father, but a sign
To love the force that grows us, to give back
What in Thy palm is senselessness and mud?
Knead, knead the substance of our understanding
Which must be beautiful in flesh to walk,
That if Thou take me angrily in hand
And hurl me to the shark, I shall not die!

LORD, I HAVE SEEN TOO MUCH

Lord, I have seen too much for one who sat
In quiet at his window's luminous eye
And puzzled over house and street and sky,
Safe only in the narrowest habitat;
Who studied peace as if the world were flat,
The edge of nature linear and dry,
But faltered at each brilliant entity
Drawn like a prize from some magician's hat.

Too suddenly this lightning is disclosed:
Lord, in a day the vacuum of Hell,
The mouth of blood, the ocean's ragged jaw,
More than embittered Adam ever saw
When driven from Eden to the East to dwell,
The lust of godhead hideously exposed!

LOVE FOR A HAND

Two hands lie still, the hairy and the white,
And soon down ladders of reflected light
The sleepers climb in silence. Gradually
They separate on paths of long ago,
Each winding on his arm the unpleasant clew
That leads, live as a nerve, to memory.

But often when too steep her dream descends,
Perhaps to the grotto where her father bends
To pick her up, the husband wakes as though
He had forgotten something in the house.
Motionless he eyes the room that glows
With the little animals of light that prowl

This way and that. Soft are the beasts of light
But softer still her hand that drifts so white
Upon the whiteness. How like a water-plant
It floats upon the black canal of sleep,
Suspended upward from the distant deep
In pure achievement of its lovely want!

Quietly then he plucks it and it folds
And is again a hand, small as a child's.
He would revive it but it barely stirs
And so he carries it off a little way
And breaks it open gently. Now he can see
The sweetness of the fruit, his hand eats hers.

MAGICIAN

Tall in his top hat, tall and alone in the room
Of aerial music, electric light
And the click of tables, the mephistophelian man
Toys with a wand and the wonders happen—for whom
And to what end the gleam of the shellacked
Trick within trick, as plain as black and white,
And all too clever, all too matter-of-fact
Like the sudden neatness of a shutting fan?

And somewhat sinister, like a millionaire
Or a poet or a street-corner quack
With a dollar bottle of cure . . . We are drawn to his eye
Only to stop at the eye we dare not dare;
We suspect and believe; *he* looks us out of face
And seems to say that magic is the knack
Of showing the result without a trace
Of the cause, end without means, what without why.

If now the amusing audience could see
His mangey unicorn that crops
The shabby velvet of his weariness,
An inch from the abyss of villainy,
The applause would freeze, the dust settle like snow,
And long before the asbestos curtain drops
Even the children would get up to go,
Be sick in the lobby, sob with young distress;

But fortunately they cannot. We proceed
Beyond the fire-eating, doves,
Padlocks, confetti, disappearing ropes,
To personal murder, the necessary deed
Of sawing a woman in half. We want her heart.
The sable executioner in gloves
Labors, but hoc est corpus! quite apart
She stands; we applaud our disappointed hopes.

And backstage somewhere, peeling his moustache,
He muses that he is an honest man

And wonders dramatically why. Deep in his ear
At times there sounds the subterranean plash
Of Alf and Phlegeton where tides revolve
With eyes of evil. There he first began;
There is the task he can no longer solve
But only wait for till his dying year.

MELBOURNE

The planted palms will keep the city warm
In any winter, and the toy Yarra flow
With boats and lovers down the grass. From walls
The flowers spring to sack the very streets
And wrought-iron tendrils curl upon the air.
The family's sex is English, and all their pain
More moderate than a long-expected death.

Yet the lipstick is poor, the girls consent
To lose their teeth and hips, and language whines
Raising the pitch to shrill humility.
At five o'clock the pubs roar on the world
And milk bars trickle pardon, as the mobs
Lunge, worse than Chicago, for the trains
Dispersing life to gardens and to tea.

Also in suburbs there is want of vice,
And even the dogs are well-behaved and nice.
Who has extracted violence like the fang,
Leaving in early minds the simile
Castration? Who watching at night the film
Suffers the technicolor King to spread
Exalted, motionless, into their dream?

For blue and diluted is this nation's eye,
Wind-worn with herding and great distances
That were not made for cities. This was a land
Laid for the park of loneliness of Earth,
And giant imagination and despair.
Who reared this sweet metropolis abides
By his own error, more profound than war.

Only my love can spare the wasted race
That worships sullenly the sordid sheep.
She shall be governor with her golden hair!
And teach the landscape laughter and destroy
With her free naked foot the matchwood quay:
Buildings themselves shall topple where she dances
And leap like frogs into the uproarious sea!

MIDNIGHT SHOW

The year is done, the last act of the vaudeville,
The last top hat and patent leather tappity-tap
Enclosed in darkness. Pat. Blackout. Only the organ
Groans, groans, its thousand golden throats in love;
While blue lowlight suffuses mysteries of sleep
Through racks of heads, and smoothly parts the gauzy veil
That slips, the last pretense of peace, into the wings.

With a raucous crash the music rises to its feet,
And pouring from the hidden eye like God the Light
The light white-molten cold fills out the vacant field
With shattered cities, striped ships, and maps with lines
That crawl—symbols of horror, symbols of obscenity;
A girl astride a giant cannon, holding a flag;
Removal of stone and stained glass saints from a known
cathedral.

And the Voice, the loving and faithful pointer, trots beside
Reel after reel, taking death in its well-trained stride.
The Voice, the polite, the auctioneer, places his hints
Like easy bids. The lab assistant, the Voice, dips
Their pity like litmus papers into His rancid heart.—
Dream to be surfeited, nerves clogged up with messages,
And, backed up at the ganglion, the news refused.

Dream to be out in snow where every corner Santa,
Heart of one generation's dreams, tinkles a bell.
We know him too. He is the Unemployed, but clowns
As the Giver, receiving pennies in a cast-iron pot.
Dream to be cold with Byrd at the world's bottom. Dream
To be warm in the Vatican, photographing a manuscript.
Dream to be there, a cell in Europe's poisoned blood.

Revulsion cannot rouse our heads for pride or protest.
The eye sees as the camera, a clean moronic gaze,
And to go is not impossible but merely careless.

O wife, what shall we tell the children that we saw?
O son, what shall we tell our father? And O my friend,
What shall we tell our senses when the lights go up
And noiselessly the golden curtains crash together!

THE MINUTE

The office building treads the marble dark,
The mother-clock with wide and golden dial
Suffers and glows. Now is the hour of birth
Of the tremulous egg. Now is the time of correction.
O midnight, zero of eternity,
Soon on a million bureaus of the city
Will lie the new-born minute.

The new-born minute on the bureau lies,
Scratching the glass with infant kick, cutting
With diamond cry the crystal and expanse
Of timelessness. This pretty tick of death
Etches its name upon the air. I turn
Titanically in distant sleep, expelling
From my lungs the bitter gas of life.

The loathsome minute grows in length and strength,
Bending its spring to forge an iron hour
That rusts from link to link, the last one bright,
The late one dead. Between the shining works
Range the clean angels, studying that tick
Like a strange dirt, but will not pick it up
Nor move it gingerly out of harm's way.

An angel is stabbed and is carried aloft howling,
For devils have gathered on a ruby jewel
Like red mites on a berry; others arrive
To tend the points with oil and smooth the heat.
See how their vicious faces, lit with sweat,
Worship the train of wheels; see how they pull
The tape-worm Time from nothing into thing.

I with my distant heart lie wide awake
Smiling at that Swiss-perfect engine room
Driven by tiny evils. Knowing no harm
Even of gongs that loom and move in towers
And hands as high as iron masts, I sleep,
At which sad sign the angels in a flock
Rise and sweep past me, spinning threads of fear.

MONGOLIAN IDIOT

A dog that spoke, a monster born of sheep
We mercilessly kill, and kill the thought,
Yet house the parrot and let the centaur go,
These being to their nature and those not.
We laugh at apes, that never quite succeed
        At eating soup or wearing hats.

Adam had named so many but not this,
This that would name a curse when it had come,
Unfinished man, or witch, or myth, or sin,
Not ever father and never quite a son.
Ape had outstripped him, dog and darling lamb
        And all the kindergarten beasts.

Enter the bare room of his mind and count
His store of words with letters large and black;
See how he handles clumsily those blocks
With swans and sums; his colored picture books.
At thirty-five he squeals to see the ball
        Bounce in the air and roll away.

Pity and fear we give this innocent
Who maimed his mother's beautiful instinct;
But she would say, "My body had a dog;
I bore the ape and nursed the crying sheep.
He is my kindness and my splendid gift
        Come from all life and for all life."

MY GRANDMOTHER

My grandmother moves to my mind in context of sorrow
And, as if apprehensive of near death, in black;
Whether erect in chair, her dry and corded throat harangued by grief,
Or at ragged book bent in Hebrew prayer,
Or gentle, submissive, and in tears to strangers;
Whether in sunny parlor or back of drawn blinds.

Though time and tongue made any love disparate,
On daguerreotype with classic perspective
Beauty I sigh and soften at is hers.
I pity her life of deaths, the agony of her own,
But most that history moved her through
Stranger lands and many houses,
Taking her exile for granted, confusing
The tongues and tasks of her children's children.

NECROPOLIS

Even in death they prosper; even in the death
Where lust lies senseless and pride fallow
The mouldering owners of rents and labor
Prosper and improve the high hill.

For theirs is the stone whose name is deepest cut,
Theirs the facsimile temple, theirs
The iron acanthus and the hackneyed Latin,
The boxwood rows and all the birds.

And even in death the poor are thickly herded
In intimate congestion under streets and alleys.
Look at the standard sculpture, the cheap
Synonymous slabs, the machined crosses.

Yes, even in death the cities are unplanned.
The heirs govern from the old centers;
They will not remove. And the ludicrous angels,
Remains of the poor, will never fly
But only multiply in the green grass.

THE NEW RING

The new ring oppresses the finger, embarrasses the hand, encumbers the whole arm. The free hand moves to cover the new ring, except late-at-night when the mouth reaches to kiss the soft silver, a sudden thought.

In the lodge of marriage, the secret society of love, the perfect circle binds and separates, moves and is stationary.

Till the ring becomes the flesh, leaving a white trench, and the finger is immune. For the brand is assumed. Till the flesh of the encumbered hand grows over the ring, as living wood over and around the iron spike. Till the value of the reason of the gift is coinworn, and the wound heals.

And until the wound heals, the new ring is a new nail driven through the hand upon the living wood, and the body hangs from the nail, and the nail holds.

NIGGER

And did ever a man go black with sun in a Belgian swamp,
On a feathery African plain where the sunburnt lioness lies,
And a cocoanut monkey grove where the cockatoos scratch
the skies,
And the zebras striped with moonlight grasses gaze and
stomp?

With a swatch of the baboon's crimson bottom cut for a lip,
And a brace of elephant ivories hung for a tusky smile,
With the muscles as level and lazy and long as the lifting
Nile,
And a penis as loaded and supple and limp as the slaver's
whip?

Are you beautiful still when you walk downtown in a knife-
cut coat
And your yellow shoes dance at the corner curb like a
brand new car,
And the buck with the arching pick looks over the new-laid
tar
As you cock your eye like a cuckoo bird on a two-o'clock
note?

When you got so little in steel-rim specs, when you taught
that French,
When you wrote that book and you made that speech in the
bottom south,
When you beat that fiddle and sang that role for Othello's
mouth,
When you blew that horn for the shirt-sleeve mob and the
snaky wench?

When you boxed that hun, when you raped that trash that
you didn't rape,
When you caught that slug with a belly of fire and a face of
gray,

When you felt that loop and you took that boot from a KKK,
And your hands hung down and your face went out in a blast of grape?

Did the Lord say yes, did the Lord say no, did you ask the Lord
When the jaw came down, when the cotton blossomed out of your bones?
Are you coming to peace, O Booker T. Lincoln Roosevelt Jones,
And is Jesus riding to raise your wage and to cut that cord?

NOSTALGIA

My soul stands at the window of my room,
And I ten thousand miles away;
My days are filled with Ocean's sound of doom,
Salt and cloud and the bitter spray.
Let the wind blow, for many a man shall die.

My selfish youth, my books with gilded edge,
Knowledge and all gaze down the street;
The potted plants upon the window ledge
Gaze down with selfish lives and sweet.
Let the wind blow, for many a man shall die.

My night is now her day, my day her night,
So I lie down, and so I rise;
The sun burns close, the star is losing height,
The clock is hunted down the skies.
Let the wind blow, for many a man shall die.

Truly a pin can make the memory bleed,
A word explode the inward mind
And turn the skulls and flowers never freed
Into the air, no longer blind.
Let the wind blow, for many a man shall die.

Laughter and grief join hands. Always the heart
Clumps in the breast with heavy stride;
The face grows lined and wrinkled like a chart,
The eyes bloodshot with tears and tide.
Let the wind blow, for many a man shall die.

OCTOBER 1

That season when the leaf deserts the bole
And half-dead see-saws through the October air
Falling face-downward on the walks to print
The decalcomania of its little soul—
Hardly has the milkman's sleepy horse
On wooden shoes echoed across the blocks,
When with its back jaws open like a dredge
The van comes lumbering up the curb to someone's door and knocks.

And four black genii muscular and shy
Holding their shy caps enter the first room
Where someone hurriedly surrenders up
The thickset chair, the mirror half awry,
Then to their burdens stoop without a sound.
One with his bare hands rends apart the bed,
One stuffs the china-barrel with stale print,
Two bear the sofa toward the door with dark funereal tread.

The corner lamp, the safety eye of night,
Enveloped in the sun blinks and goes blind
And soon the early risers pick their way
Through kitchenware and pillows bolt upright.
The bureau on the sidewalk with bare back
And wrinkling veneer is most disgraced,
The sketch of Paris suffers in the wind,
Only the bike, its nose against the wall, does not show haste.

Two hours—the movers mop their necks and look,
Filing through dust and echoes back and forth.
The halls are hollow and all the floors are cleared
Bare to the last board, to the most secret nook;
But on the street a small chaos survives
That slowly now the leviathan ingests,
And schoolboys and stenographers stare at
The truck, the house, the husband in his hat who stands and rests.

He turns with miserable expectant face
And for the last time enters. On the wall
A picture-stain spreads from the nail-hole down.
Each object live and dead has left its trace.
He leaves his key; but as he quickly goes
This question comes behind: Did someone die?
Is someone rich or poor, better or worse?
What shall uproot a house and bring this care into his eye?

THE PHENOMENON

How lovely it was, after the official fright,
To walk in the shadowy drifts, as if the clouds
Saturated with the obscurity of night
Had died and fallen piecemeal into shrouds.

What crepes there were, what sables heaped on stones,
What soft shakos on posts, tragically gay!
And oil-pool flooded fields that blackly shone
The more black under the liquid eye of day!

It was almost warmer to the touch than sands
And sweeter-tasting than the white, and yet
Walking, the children held their fathers' hands
Like visitors to a mine or parapet.

Then black it snowed again and while it fell
You could see the sun, an irritated rim
Wheeling through smoke; each from his shallow hell
Experienced injured vision growing dim.

But one day all was clear, and one day soon,
Sooner than those who witnessed it had died,
Nature herself forgot the phenomenon,
Her faulty snowfall brilliantly denied.

PIANO

The perfect ice of the thin keys must break
And fingers crash through stillness into sound,
And through the mahogany darkness of the lake
Splinter the muteness where all notes are found.
O white face floating upwards amidst hair!
Sweet hands entangled in the golden snare,
Escape, escape, escape,
Or in the coils of joy be drowned.

What is the cabinet that holds such speech
And is obedient to caresses strange
As tides that stroke the long-deserted beach,
And gales that scourge the Peruvian mountain range?
O flesh of wood with flanks aglow with suns,
O quivering as at the burst of monstrous guns,
Subside, subside, subside,
Or into dust and atoms change.

Nor can the note-shaped heart, nor can the ear
Withstand your praise, O numbers more appalling
Than ringed and voyaging on the atmosphere
Those heavy flocks of fallen angels falling;
You strike with fists of heaven against the void
Where all but choiring music is destroyed,
And light, and light, and light,
Bursts into voice forever calling.

POET

Il arrive que l'esprit demande la poesie

Left leg flung out, head cocked to the right,
Tweed coat or army uniform, with book,
Beautiful eyes, who is this walking down?
Who, glancing at the pane of glass looks sharp
And thinks it is not he—as when a poet
Comes swiftly on some half-forgotten poem
And loosely holds the page, steady of mind,
            Thinking it is not his?

And when will *you* exist?—Oh, it is I,
Incredibly skinny, stooped, and neat as pie,
Ignorant as dirt, erotic as an ape,
Dreamy as puberty—with dirty hair!
Into the room like kangaroo he bounds,
Ears flopping like the most expensive hound's;
His chin receives all questions as he bows
            Mouthing a green bon-bon.

Has no more memory than rubber. Stands
Waist-deep in heavy mud of thought and broods
At his own wetness. When he would get out,
To his surprise he lifts in air a phrase
As whole and clean and silvery as a fish
Which jumps and dangles on his damned hooked grin,
But like a name-card on a man's lapel
            Calls him a conscious fool.

And child-like he remembers all his life
And cannily constructs it, fact by fact,
As boys paste postage stamps in careful books,
Denoting pence and legends and profiles,
Nothing more valuable.—And like a thief,
His eyes glassed over and congealed with guilt,
Fondles his secrets like a case of tools,
            And waits in empty doors.

By men despised for knowing what he is,
And by himself. But he exists for women.
As dolls to girls, as perfect wives to men,
So he to women. And to himself a thing,
All ages, epicene, without a trade.
To girls and wives always alive and fated;
To men and scholars always dead like Greek
And always mistranslated.

Towards exile and towards shame he lures himself,
Tongue winding on his arm, and thinks like Eve
By biting apple will become most wise.
Sentio ergo sum: he feels his way
And words themselves stand up for him like Braille
And punch and perforate his parchment ear.
All language falls like Chinese on his soul,
Image of song unsounded.

This is the coward's coward that in his dreams
Sees shapes of pain grow tall. Awake at night
He peers at sounds and stumbles at a breeze.
And none holds life less dear. For as a youth
Who by some accident observes his love
Naked and in some natural ugly act,
He turns with loathing and with flaming hands,
Seared and betrayed by sight.

He is the business man, on beauty trades,
Dealer in arts and thoughts who, like the Jew,
Shall rise from slums and hated dialects
A tower of bitterness. Shall be always strange,
Hunted and then sought after. Shall be sat
Like an ambassador from another race
At tables rich with music. He shall eat flowers,
Chew honey and spit out gall. They shall all smile
And love and pity him.

His death shall be by drowning. In that hour
When the last bubble of pure heaven's air
Hovers within his throat, safe on his bed,
A small eternal figurehead in terror,
He shall cry out and clutch his days of straw
Before the blackest wave. Lastly, his tomb
Shall list and founder in the troughs of grass
And none shall speak his name.

THE POTOMAC

The thin Potomac scarcely moves
But to divide Virginia from today;
Rider, whichever is your way
You go due south and neither South improves;
Not this, of fractured columns and queer rents
And rags that charm the nationalist,
Not that, the axle of the continents,
Nor the thin sky that flows unprejudiced
This side and that, cleansing the poisoned breath.

For Thomas died a Georgian death
And now the legion bones of Arlington
Laid out in marble alphabets
Stare on the great tombs of the capitol
Where heroes calcified and cool
Ponder the soldier named Unknown
Whose lips are guarded with live bayonets.

Yet he shall speak though sentries walk
And columns with their cold Corinthian stalk
Shed gold-dust pollen on Brazil
To turn the world to Roman chalk;
Yet he shall speak, yet he shall speak
Whose sulphur lit the flood-lit Dome,
Whose hands were never in the kill,
Whose will was furrows of Virginia loam.

But not like London blown apart by boys
Who learned the books of love in English schools,
His name shall strike the fluted columns down;
These shall lie buried deep as fifty Troys,
The money fade like leaves from green to brown,
And embassies dissolve to molecules.

THE PROGRESS OF FAUST

He was born in Deutschland, as you would suspect,
And graduated in magic from Cracow
In Fifteen Five. His portraits show a brow
Heightened by science. The eye is indirect,
As of bent light upon a crooked soul,
And that he bargained with the Prince of Shame
For pleasures intellectually foul
Is known by every court that lists his name.

His frequent disappearances are put down
To visits in the regions of the damned
And to the periodic deaths he shammed,
But, unregenerate and in Doctor's gown,
He would turn up to lecture at the fair
And do a minor miracle for a fee.
Many a life he whispered up the stair
To teach the black art of anatomy.

He was as deaf to angels as an oak
When, in the fall of Fifteen Ninety-four,
He went to London and crashed through the floor
In mock damnation of the playgoing folk.
Weekending with the scientific crowd,
He met Sir Francis Bacon and helped draft
"Colours of Good and Evil" and read aloud
An obscene sermon at which no one laughed.

He toured the Continent for a hundred years
And subsidized among the peasantry
The puppet play, his tragic history;
With a white glove he boxed the devil's ears
And with a black his own. Tired of this,
He published penny poems about his sins,
In which he placed the heavy emphasis
On the white glove which, for a penny, wins.

Some time before the hemmorhage of the Kings
Of France, he turned respectable and taught;

Quite suddenly everything that he had thought
Seemed to grow scholars' beards and angels' wings.
It was the Overthrow. On Reason's throne
He sat with the fair Phrygian on his knees
And called all universities his own,
As plausible a figure as you please.

Then back to Germany as the sages' sage
To preach comparative science to the young
Who came from every land in a great throng
And knew they heard the master of the age.
When for a secret formula he paid
The Devil another fragment of his soul,
His scholars wept, and several even prayed
That Satan would restore him to them whole.

Backwardly tolerant, Faustus was expelled
From the Third Reich in Nineteen Thirty-nine.
His exit caused the breaching of the Rhine,
Except for which the frontier might have held.
Five years unknown to enemy and friend
He hid, appearing on the sixth to pose
In an American desert at war's end
Where, at his back, a dome of atoms rose.

RECAPITULATIONS

I

I was born downtown on a wintry day
And under the roof where Poe expired;
Tended by nuns my mother lay
Dark-haired and beautiful and tired.

Doctors and cousins paid their call,
The rabbi and my father helped.
A crucifix burned on the wall
Of the bright room where I was whelped.

At one week all my family prayed,
Stuffed wine and cotton in my craw;
The rabbi blessed me with a blade
According to the Mosaic Law.

The white steps blazed in Baltimore
And cannas and white statuary.
I went home voluble and sore
Influenced by Abraham and Mary.

II

At one the Apocalypse had spoken,
Von Moltke fell, I was housebroken.

At two how could I understand
The murder of Archduke Ferdinand?

France was involved with history,
I with my thumbs when I was three.

A sister came, we neared a war,
Paris was shelled when I was four.

I joined in our peach-kernel drive
For poison gas when I was five.

At six I cheered the big parade,
Burned sparklers and drank lemonade.

At seven I passed at school though I
Was far too young to say *Versailles.*

At eight the boom began to tire,
I tried to set our house on fire.

The Bolsheviks had drawn the line,
Lenin was striken, I was nine.

—What evils do not retrograde
To my first odious decade?

III

Saints by whose pages I would swear,
    My Zarathustra, Edward Lear,
Ulysses, Werther, fierce Flaubert,
    Where are my books of yesteryear?

Sixteen and sixty are a pair;
    We twice live by philosophies;
My marginalia of the hair,
    Are you at one with Socrates?

Thirty subsides yet does not dare,
    Sixteen and sixty bang their fists.
How is it that I no longer care
    For Kant and the Transcendentalists?

Public libraries lead to prayer,
    EN APXH ἦν ὁ λόγος—still
Eliot and John are always there
    To tempt our admirari nil.

IV

I lived in a house of panels,
    Victorian, darkly made;

A virgin in bronze and marble
    Leered from the balustrade.

The street was a tomb of virtues,
    Autumnal for dreams and haunts;
I gazed from the polished windows
    Toward a neighborhood of aunts.

Mornings I practiced piano,
    Wrote elegies and sighed;
The evenings were conversations
    Of poetry and suicide.

Weltschmerz and mysticism,
    What tortures we undergo!
I loved with the love of Heinrich
    And the poison of Edgar Poe.

V

My first small book was nourished in the dark,
Secretly written, published, and inscribed.
Bound in wine-red, it made no brilliant mark.
Rather impossible relatives subscribed.

The best review was one I wrote myself
Under the name of a then-dearest friend.
Two hundred volumes stood upon my shelf
Saying my golden name from end to end.

I was not proud but seriously stirred;
Sorrow was song and money poetry's maid!
Sorrow I had in many a ponderous word,
But were the piper and the printer paid?

VI

The third-floor thoughts of discontented youth
Once saw the city, hardened against truth,

Get set for war. He coupled a last rime
And waited for the summons to end time.

It came. The box-like porch where he had sat,
The four bright boxes of a medium flat,
Chair he had sat in, glider where he lay
Reading the poets and prophets of his day,

He assigned abstractly to his dearest friend,
Glanced at the little street hooked at the end,
The line of poplars lately touched with spring,
Lovely as Laura, breathless, beckoning.

Mother was calm, until he left the door;
The trolley passed his sweetheart's house before
She was awake. The Armory was cold,
But naked, shivering, shocked he was enrolled.

It was the death he never quite forgot
Through the four years of death, and like as not
The true death of the best of all of us
Whose present life is largely posthumous.

VII

We waged a war within a war,
    A cause within a cause;
The glory of it was withheld
    In keeping with the laws
Whereby the public need not know
The pitfalls of the status quo.

Love was the reason for the blood:
    The black men of our land
Were seen to walk with pure white girls
    Laughing and hand in hand.
This most unreasonable state
No feeling White would tolerate.

We threw each other from the trams,
    We carried knives and pipes,
We sacrificed in self-defense
    Some of the baser types,
But though a certain number died
You would not call it fratricide.

The women with indignant tears
    Professed to love the Blacks,
And dark and wooly heads still met
    With heads of English flax.
Only the cockney could conceive
Of any marriage so naïve.

Yet scarcely fifty years before
    Their fathers rode to shoot
The undressed aborigines,
    Though not to persecute.
A fine distinction lies in that
They have no others to combat.

By order of the high command
    The black men were removed
To the interior and north;
    The crisis thus improved,
Even the women could detect
Their awful fall from intellect.

VIII

I plucked the bougainvillaea
    In Queensland in time of war;
The train stopped at the station
    And I reached it from my door.

I have never kept a flower
    And this one I never shall
I thought as I laid the blossom
    In the leaves of *Les Fleurs du Mal.*

I read my book in the desert
    In the time of death and fear,
The flower slipped from the pages
    And fell to my lap, my dear.

I sent it inside my letter,
    The purplest kiss I knew,
And thus you abused my passion
    With "A most Victorian Jew."

RED INDIAN

To Jim Powell

Purest of breed of all the tribes
That trekked from time and took the Trail of Tears
There to the plain beyond the bribes
Of best advantage, past the rifle's reach,
Where instinct rests and action disappears
And the skulls of cattle bleach.

High in the plateaus of their soul
The silence is reshaped like rocks by wind,
Their eyes are beads that pay their toll,
Record the race-long heritage of grief,
At altitudes where memory is thinned,
Frown like a wrinkled chief.

The painted feather still upright
They walk in concrete Tulsa dark and mute,
Their bravest blankets slashing bright
The afternoon of progress and of wives;
Their children glow like some primordial fruit
Cut from the branch by knives.

Bark-smooth as spears and arrow-straight
They watch the world like winter trees and grow;
Forests of them revive and wait,
In timeless hibernation dream and stir.
These are the lives that love the soundless snow
And wear the wind like fur.

Because their pride of nation leaps,
The august rivers where they yelled and died
Move with a blood that never sleeps.
Because their nature suffers the arrest
Of seed, their silence crowds us like a tide
And moves their mournful quest.

A ROBBERY

By day I had dispraised their life,
Accused foremost the little cheated wives
Whose hands like trailers ludicrously hitched
To husbands, over the graph of business bump.
As often, with my friend, I laughed at them,
All but their young, whose strenuous anarchy
Asked Why and promised war.

So of their legal dark of nights,
And bed revenge, and competent small births
That shut us out from marriage, I despaired:
Men brought home hate like evening papers, maids
Longed for their slums, the inarticulate clock
Spoke once, and faces, double-locked and still,
Turned to the wall to sleep.

I show that fear unearthed that Boy.
Into the taut membrane of night, like knives
A woman screams, rending with rape our rest.
Bodies are ripped from beds; the snapped dream hangs:
And quick to plunge the torn portieres of sleep
We race soft-running Horror the length of halls.
Ghouls are at every door.

Down in the hostile dark, as one,
The heavy faces point, close in, take aim,
And hands describe centripetal broad Wheels
Through which unseen a wiry robber moves.
Voices enlarge, cops clamber from the sky,
Our sudden symmetry dissolves. We laugh.
"Nothing is caught, or lost."

Yet our emergency is lost,
Which would have, naked in the domestic night,
Brought us like actual murder to relief.
Boys have mixed blood and kissed to seal an oath.
Boys have an oath. O we were close to boys,

The salesman, the real estator, the clerk, and I,
Their enemy, their poet.

Robber, paid agent of our hate,
I kiss my hand to you across the roofs
And jungle of back alleys where you hide.
You with your guns are like a boy I loved.
He was born dead and never had a name.
He was my little son. Night took him off.
Hard to unlearn is love.

SATIRE: ANXIETY

Alas, I would be overloved,
A sign, a Wonder unreproved,
A bronze colossus standing high
As Rhodes or famous Liberty,
Bridging with my almighty thighs
A stainless steel metropolis
Where pigmy men in clothing creep
To Lilliputian work and sleep,
And Love with microscopic tears
Whispers to wee and perfect ears.
I would obscure the sun and throw
A shadow with my smallest toe
That down their teeming canyon files
Time could be told a hundred miles;
Lightning would flash within my hand,
An airman's beacon and sign of land,
My eyes eclipse the polar star,
Aldebaran and the flare of war;
Golden my head and cleanly hewn
Would sail above the lesser moon
And dart above the Pleiades
To peer at new astronomies
From where the earth, a bluish clod,
Seems smallest in the eye of God.

But when in lucid morning I
Survey my bulk and history,
Composite fool alive in air
With caecum and vestigial hair,
A thing of not-too-godly form
Conversant with the waiting worm,
Fixed in a span between two shades
For four or five or six decades,
Then all my pride and all my hope
As backward through a telescope
Diminish: I walk an endless street
Where topless towers for height compete,

And men of wiser blood and bone
Destroy me for the things they own—
Their taxes, vital tubes, and sons
Submissive in a world of guns.
I see my hands grow small and clear
Until they wink and disappear.

SCYROS

snuffle and sniff and handkerchief

The doctor punched my vein
The captain called me Cain
Upon my belly sat the sow of fear
With coins on either eye
The President came by
And whispered to the braid what none could hear

High over where the storm
Stood steadfast cruciform
The golden eagle sank in wounded wheels
White Negroes laughing still
Crept fiercely on Brazil
Turning the navies upward on their keels

Now one by one the trees
Stripped to their naked knees
To dance upon the heaps of shrunken dead
The roof of England fell
Great Paris tolled her bell
And China staunched her milk and wept for bread

No island singly lay
But lost its name that day
The Ainu dived across the plunging sands
From dawn to dawn to dawn
King George's birds came on
Strafing the tulips from his children's hands

Thus in the classic sea
Southeast from Thessaly
The dynamited mermen washed ashore
And tritons dressed in steel
Trolled heads with rod and reel
And dredged potatoes from the Aegean floor

Hot is the sky and green
Where Germans have been seen
The moon leaks metal on the Atlantic fields
Pink boys in birthday shrouds
Loop lightly through the clouds
Or coast the peaks of Finland on their shields

That prophet year by year
Lay still but could not hear
Where scholars tapped to find his new remains
Gog and Magog ate pork
In vertical New York
And war began next Wednesday on the Danes

THE SECOND-BEST BED

In the name of the almighty God, amen,
  I, William Shakespeare, take my pen
  And do bequeath in perfect health
To Christ my soul and to my kin my wealth
    When I am dead.
    And to Anne, good dame,
    I bequeath my name,
A table, a chair, and the second-best bed.

To Judith a hundred fifty pounds I give,
  The same if three more years she live,
  And the broad-edge silver bowl. To Joan
My hose and clothes and all the suits I own
    Both blue and red.
    And to Anne, good dame,
    I bequeath my name,
A table, a chair, and the second-best bed.

Ten pounds to beggars for their drink and board,
  To Mr. Thomas Cole my sword,
  To Richard Burbage, Cundell, Nash,
Heminge and Hamlet one pound six in cash,
    And to her I wed
    Who is Anne, good dame,
    I bequeath my name,
A table, a chair, and the second-best bed.

To Joan also my Stratford house I will,
  For sisters shall not go with nil,
  And to her sons five pounds apiece
To be paid within a year of my decease.
    And as I have said
    To Anne, good dame,
    I bequeath my name,
A table, a chair, and the second-best bed.

Last, to my daughter, born Susanna Hall,
  My barns and stables, lands and all,

Tenements, orchards, jewels, and wares,
And these forever for herself and heirs,
Till all are dead;
But to Anne, good dame,
I bequeath my name,
A table, a chair, and the second-best bed.

Good wife, bad fortune is to blame
That I bequeath, when I am dead,
To you my honor and my name,
A table, a chair, and the second-best bed.

SIX RELIGIOUS LYRICS

I

I sing the simplest flower,
The earliest quest of day,
That wears in its white corolla
The signet of breathing May.

For the envelope of beauty
Discloses the female part,
The bending and swollen stigma,
The sly tongue of the heart.

And the dusty bee for nectar
Enters and drinks his fill,
And the wind comes freely, freshly
To assist the season's will.

I give you the simplest flower,
The color of air, a dress
Self-woven and frail and holy,
The signet of love's distress.

II

Upstairs the shuttles of the loom
Ravel and weave the shadow-play;
Downstairs on endless steps of gloom
Those souls in sorrowful array . . .

Gentlest decline of inward hills
That distance lightens and makes fair,
Valley of instruments that fills
The sibylline nocturnal air!

What innuendo of their cry
Will enter life and course the blood,
That gods and goddesses so high
May represent our earthly good?

What human kiss can take the place
Of these of such gigantic scope;
What joy describe the human face
Washed down the street in floods of hope?

III

Dark words, birds of the race
    That voyage time and birth
To pierce the columns of the East,
    Fossils of prayer and earth:

Grave words, words of the name
    That live from face to face,
Remembering love's antiquity,
    Exile and dead disgrace;

Iron words, oaths of the war,
    Seed of the seed of Cain,
Under whose mail and metal dew
    Our thousand youths are lain;

Is Babel there, fallen of heart,
    Unfinished on the sky,
Can speech renew the tribe of joy
    And Jesus justify?

IV

The soldier's death occasions
Seldom a bitter cry:
We feel in his abrasions
A death that we deny.

To fall as such another
And hundreds far and near
Is true for friend and brother,
But false for us who fear.

Luck has a wider cover
Than Justice's or God's;
Our chances scarcely hover,
The Exception sees and nods.

Saluting the death of any
The mass will seldom grieve,
For out of the fall of many
The one will rise and leave.

V

Treasure your anonymity,
You who remain, however torn,
Eldest of us and best of us,
Die silent and be silent born.

At length the elected must subside,
The honorable and the traitor kind,
And armies all repose in clay,
Corpses and booty left behind.

Inviolable and sacred mass,
You were not good but good enough,
You nodded at your destinies,
The last and next-to-last rebuff.

Nation and race and family
Have built on many a smoking town;
Samson was also slightly blind
But brought the roof of Dagon down.

VI

for L. Q.

Witty of heart and pure of heart,
    In churches cavernous and dim
You drank the cup of Christ apart
    And knelt and worshipped Him.

Somewhere I waited for your arm
    And walked the traffic of broad day
Sadly, for all the earthly harm
    From which you turned to pray.

In cloisters where your sisters dwelled
    You walked in peace and dreamed to die;
You did not take the veil they held,
    The kiss to sanctify,

But pleasantly amongst us all
    Who doubt and shout and depredate
Live by the charity of Paul
    And keep the silent gate.

THE SNOB

At what time in its little history
Did on the matrix of his brain a blow
Fall that struck like a relentless die
And left him speechless; or was it by degrees
That the algid folds of mind, caught in a pose,
        Hardened and set like concrete,
Printing and fixing a distorted moment?

Nothing but death will smash this ugly cast
That wears its trade mark big upon its face,
A scutcheon for Greek-letter brotherhoods
Where it is weakly sworn by smiles to cow
Unequals, niggers or just Methodists.
        His bearing is a school of thought,
But he is not funny and not unimportant.

THE SOUTHERNER

He entered with the authority of politeness
And the jokes died in the air. A well-made blaze
Grew round the main log in the fireplace
Spontaneously. I watched its brightness
Spread to the altered faces of my guests.
They did not like the Southerner. I did.
A liberal felt that someone should forbid
That soft voice making its soft arrests.

As when a Negro or a prince extends
His hand to an average man, and the mind
Speeds up a minute and then drops behind,
So did the conversation of my friends.
I was amused by this respectful awe
Which those hotly deny who have no prince.
I watched the frown, the stare, and the wince
Recede into attention, the arms thaw.

I saw my southern evil memories
Raped from my mind before my eyes, my youth
Practicing caste, perfecting the untruth
Of staking honor on the wish to please.
I saw my honor's paradox:
Grandpa, the saintly Jew, keeping his beard
In difficult Virginia, yet endeared
Of blacks and farmers, although orthodox.

The nonsense of the gracious lawn,
The fall of hollow columns in the pines,
Do these deceive more than the rusted signs
Of Jesus on the road? Can they go on
In the timeless manner of all gentlefolk
There in a culture rotted and unweeded
Where the black yoni of the South is seeded
By crooked men in denims thin as silk?

They do go on, denying still the fall
Of Richmond and man, who gently live

On the street above the violence, fugitive,
Graceful, and darling, who recall
The heartbroken country once about to flower,
Full of black poison, beautiful to smell,
Who know how to conform, how to compel,
And how from the best bush to receive a flower.

SYDNEY BRIDGE

Though I see you, O rainbow of iron and rivetted lace
As a dancer who leaps to the music of music and light,
And poised on the pin of the moment of marvelous grace
Holds her breath in the downfall and curve of her motionless flight;

Though you walk like a queen with the stays of your womanly steel
And the pearls of your bodice are heavy with sensual pride,
And the million come under your notice and graciously kneel,
As the navies of nations come slowly to moor at your side;

Yet your pace is the pace of a man's, and your arms are outspread
In a trick of endurance to charm the demand of the bays,
And your tendons are common—the cables are coarse on your head,

You are marxist and sweaty! You grind for the labor of days;
And O sphinx of our harbor of beauty, your banner is red
And outflung at the end of the world like a silvery phrase!

THE SYNAGOGUE

The synagogue dispirits the deep street,
Shadows the face of the pedestrian,
It is the adumbration of the Wall,
The stone survival that laments itself,
Our old entelechy of stubborn God,
Our calendar that marks a separate race.

The swift cathedral palpitates the blood,
The soul moves upward like a wing to meet
The pinnacles of saints. There flocks of thanks
In nooks of holy tracery arrive
And rested take their message in mid-air
Sphere after sphere into the papal heaven.

The altar of the Hebrews is a house,
No relic but a place, Sinai itself,
Not holy ground but factual holiness
Wherein the living god is resident.
Our scrolls are volumes of the thundered law
Sabbath by sabbath wound by hand to read.

He knows Al-Eloah to whom the Arab
Barefooted falls on sands, on table roofs,
In latticed alleys underneath the egg
On wide mosaics, when the crier shrills.
O profitable curse, most sacred rug,
Your book is blindness and your sword is rust.

And Judenhetze is the course of time;
We were rebellious, all but Abraham,
And skulked like Jonah, angry at the gourd.
Our days are captives in the minds of kings,
We stand in tens disjointed on the world
Grieving the ribbon of a coast we hated.

Some choose the ethics of belief beyond
Even particular election. Some
In bland memorial churches modify

The architecture of the state, and heaven
Disfranchised watches, caput mortuum,
The human substance eating, voting, smiling.

The Jew has no bedecked magnificat
But sits in stricken ashes after death,
Refusing grace; his grave is flowerless,
He gutters in the tallow of his name.
At Rome the multiplying tapers sing
Life endless in the history of art.

And Zion womanless refuses grace
To the first woman as to Magdalene,
But half-remembers Judith or Rahab,
The shrewd good heart of Esther honors still,
And weeps for almost sacred Ruth, but doubts
Either full harlotry or the faultless birth.

Our wine is wine, our bread is harvest bread
That feeds the body and is not the body.
Our blessing is to wine but not the blood
Nor to sangreal the sacred dish. We bless
The whiteness of the dish and bless the water
And are not anthropaphagous to him.

The immanent son then came as one of us
And stood against the ark. We have no prophets,
Our scholars are afraid. There have been friars,
Great healers, poets. The stars were terrible.
At the Sadducee court he touched our panic;
We were betrayed to sacrifice this man.

We live by virtue of philosophy,
Past love, and have our devious reward.
For faith he gave us land and took the land,
Thinking us exiles of all humankind.
Our name is yet the identity of God
That storms the falling altar of the world.

TERMINAL

Over us stands the broad electric face
With semaphores that flick into the gaps,
Notching the time on sixtieths of space,
Springing the traveller through the folded traps
Downstairs with luggage anywhere to go
While others happily toil upward too;
Well-dressed or stricken, banished or restored,
Hundreds step down and thousands get aboard.

In neat confusion, tickets in our brain
We press the hard plush to our backs and sigh;
The brakeman thumbs his watch, the children strain
The windows to their smeary sight—Goodbye,
The great car creaks, the stone wall turns away
And lights flear past like fishes undersea;
Heads rolling heavily and all as one
With languid screams we charge into the sun.

Now through the maelstrom of the town we ride
Clicking with speed like skates on solid ice;
Streets drop and buildings silently collide,
Rails spread apart, converge and neatly splice.
Through gasping blanks of air we pound and ford
Bulking our courage forward like a road,
Climbing the world on long dead-level stairs
With catwalk stilts and trestles hung by hairs.

Out where the oaks on wide turntables grow
And constellation hamlets gyre and glow,
The straight-up bridges dive and from below
The river's sweet eccentric borders flow;
Into the culverts sliced like lands of meat,
Armies of cornstalks on their ragged feet,
And upward-outward toward the blueback hill
Where clouds of thunder graze and drink their fill.

And always at our side, swifter than we
The racing rabbits of the wire lope

And in their blood the words at liberty
Outspeed themselves; but on our rail we grope
Drinking from one white wire overhead
Hot drinks of action and hell's fiery feed.
Lightly the finger-shaped antennae feel
And lightly cheer the madness of our wheel.

We turn, we turn, thrumming the harp of sounds
And all is pleasure's move, motion of joy;
Now we imagine that we go like hounds
And now like sleds and now like many a toy
Coming alive on Christmas Day to crawl
Between the great world of the floor and wall,
But on the peak of speed we flag and fall—
Fixed on the air we do not move at all.

Arrived at space we settle in our car
And stare like souls admitted to the sky;
Nothing at length is close at hand or far;
All feats of image vanish from the eye.
Upon our brow is set the bursting star,
Upon the void the wheel and axle-bar,
The planetary fragments broken lie;
Distance is dead and light can only die.

THE TINGLING BACK

Sometimes deeply immured in white-washed tower
quiet at ink and thinking book,
alone with my own smoke,
the blood at rest, the body far below,
swiftly there falls an angry shower
of arrows upon my back,
like bees or electric needles run amok
between my flesh and shirt. I know
then I have touched the pain
of amour-propre, of something yesterday
I said and I should not have said,
I did and must not do.
These needles wing their insights from my brain
and through and through my flesh they play
to prick my skin with red
letters of shame and blue blurs of tattoo.
I sweat and take my medicine
for one must be sincere
and study one's sincerity like a crime:
to be the very last to smile,
the first one to begin
(when danger streaks the atmosphere) to fear,
to pocket praises like a dime,
to pet the crocodile,
to see a foreign agony as stone,
to ravel dreams in crowded room,
to let the hair grow tall,
to skin the eye and thrust it to the wind.
Yet if I stood with God alone
inside the blinding tomb
I would not feel embarrassment at all
nor those hot needles of the mind
which are so clean. I'd ask
not if I'd known the tissue of my will
and scarified my body white,
but whether, insincere,

I'd grown to the simplicity of a mask;
and if in natural error still
whether my fingers might
destroy the true and keep the error near.

TO EVALYN FOR CHRISTMAS

Greeting the hostile parents, you or I,
With sheepish bravery like the young who know
The exact extent of every household law—
But who are man and woman, soldier and wife,

Let us again today steal to our chair
And touch like rightful people in the house
Our bodies and our deep or trivial news
And the small fortune of our startled joy.

For your great heart comes over me like sound
Of Christmas and your look and your bright arms
Balanced with packages and wreaths throw down
A heap of tokens for the world's birthday.

For Anno Domini, for the year of War
Hardness I give, a drop of medicine,
A tear to take which on your tender tongue
May be the poison or the dram of strength

To succour destiny or to destroy
The daily Christian you which is a fir
Warming the room with odours of surprise
And hung with points of light and boughs of green.

TRAVELOGUE FOR EXILES

Look and remember. Look upon this sky;
Look deep and deep into the sea-clean air,
The unconfined, the terminus of prayer.
Speak now and speak into the hallowed dome.
What do you hear? What does the sky reply?
The heavens are taken: this is not your home.

Look and remember. Look upon this sea;
Look down and down into the tireless tide.
What of a life below, a life inside,
A tomb, a cradle in the curly foam?
The waves arise; sea-wind and sea agree
The waters are taken: this is not your home.

Look and remember. Look upon this land,
Far, far across the factories and the grass.
Surely, there, surely, they will let you pass.
Speak then and ask the forest and the loam.
What do you hear? What does the land command?
The earth is taken: this is not your home.

TROOP TRAIN

It stops the town we come through. Workers raise
Their oily arms in good salute and grin.
Kids scream as at a circus. Business men
Glance hopefully and go their measured way.
And women standing at their dumbstruck door
More slowly wave and seem to warn us back,
As if a tear blinding the course of war
Might once dissolve our iron in their sweet wish.

Fruit of the world, O clustered on ourselves
We hang as from a cornucopia
In total friendliness, with faces bunched
To spray the streets with catcalls and with leers.
A bottle smashes on the moving ties
And eyes fixed on a lady smiling pink
Stretch like a rubber-band and snap and sting
The mouth that wants the drink-of-water kiss.

And on through crummy continents and days,
Deliberate, grimy, slightly drunk we crawl,
The good-bad boys of circumstance and chance,
Whose bucket-helmets bang the empty wall
Where twist the murdered bodies of our packs
Next to the guns that only seem themselves.
And distance like a strap adjusted shrinks,
Tightens across the shoulder and holds firm.

Here is a deck of cards; out of this hand
Dealer, deal me my luck, a pair of bulls,
The right draw to a flush, the one-eyed jack.
Diamonds and hearts are red but spades are black,
And spades are spades and clubs are clovers—black.
But deal me winners, souvenirs of peace.
This stands to reason and arithmetic,
Luck also travels and not all come back.

Trains lead to ships and ships to death or trains,
And trains to death or trucks, and trucks to death,

Or trucks lead to the march, the march to death,
Or that survival which is all our hope;
And death leads back to trucks and trains and ships,
But life leads to the march, O flag! at last
The place of life found after trains and death
—Nightfall of nations brilliant after war.

THE TWINS

Likeness has made them animal and shy.
See how they turn their full gaze left and right,
Seeking the other, yet not moving close;
Nothing in their relationship is gross,
But soft, conspicuous, like giraffes. And why
Do they not speak except by sudden sight?

Sisters kiss freely and unsubtle friends
Wrestle like lovers; brothers loudly laugh:
These in a dreamier bondage dare not touch.
Each is the other's soul and hears too much
The heartbeat of the other; each apprehends
The sad duality and the imperfect half.

The one lay sick, the other wandered free,
But like a child to a small plot confined
Walked a short way and dumbly reappeared.
Is it not all-in-all of what they feared,
The single death, the obvious destiny
That maims the miracle their will designed?

For they go emptily from face to face,
Keeping the instinctive partnership of birth
A ponderous marriage and a sacred name;
Theirs is the pride of shouldering each the same
The old indignity of Esau's race
And Dromio's denouement of tragic mirth.

UNIVERSITY

To hurt the Negro and avoid the Jew
Is the curriculum. In mid-September
The entering boys, identified by hats,
Wander in a maze of mannered brick
    Where boxwood and magnolia brood
    And columns with imperious stance
    Like rows of ante-bellum girls
        Eye them, outlanders.

In whited cells, on lawns equipped for peace,
Under the arch, and lofty banister,
Equals shake hands, unequals blankly pass;
The exemplary weather whispers, "Quiet, quiet"
    And visitors on tiptoe leave
    For the raw North, the unfinished West,
    As the young, detecting an advantage,
        Practice a face.

Where, on their separate hill, the colleges,
Like manor houses of an older law,
Gaze down embankments on a land in fee,
The Deans, dry spinsters over family plate,
    Ring out the English name like coin,
    Humor the snob and lure the lout.
    Within the precincts of this world
        Poise is a club.

But on the neighboring range, misty and high,
The past is absolute: some luckless race
Dull with inbreeding and conformity
Wears out its heart, and comes barefoot and bad
    For charity or jail. The scholar
    Sanctions their obsolete disease;
    The gentleman revolts with shame
        At his ancestor.

And the true nobleman, once a democrat,
Sleeps on his private mountain. He was one

Whose thought was shapely and whose dream was broad;
This school he held his art and epitaph.
    But now it takes from him his name,
    Falls open like a dishonest look,
    And shows us, rotted and endowed,
        Its senile pleasure.

V-LETTER

I love you first because your face is fair,
Because your eyes Jewish and blue,
Set sweetly with the touch of foreignness
Above the cheekbones, stare rather than dream.
Often your countenance recalls a boy
Blue-eyed and small, whose silent mischief
Tortured his parents and compelled my hate
To wish his ugly death.
Because of this reminder, my soul's trouble,
And for your face, so often beautiful,
I love you, wish you life.

I love you first because you wait, because
For your own sake, I cannot write
Beyond these words. I love you for these words
That sting and creep like insects and leave filth.
I love you for the poverty you cry
And I bend down with tears of steel
That melt your hand like wax, not for this war
The droplets shattering
Those candle-glowing fingers of my joy,
But for your name of agony, my love,
That cakes my mouth with salt.

And all your imperfections and perfections
And all your magnitude of grace
And all this love explained and unexplained
Is just a breath. I see you woman-size
And this looms larger and more goddess-like
Than silver goddesses on screens.
I see you in the ugliness of light,
Yet you are beautiful,
And in the dark of absence your full length
Is such as meets my body to the full
Though I am starved and huge.

You turn me from these days as from a scene
Out of an open window far

Where lies the foreign city and the war.
You are my home and in your spacious love
I dream to march as under flaring flags
        Until the door is gently shut.
Give me the tearless lesson of your pride,
                Teach me to live and die
As one deserving anonymity,
The mere devotion of a house to keep
                A woman and a man.

Give me the free and poor inheritance
        Of our own kind, not furniture
Of education, nor the prophet's pose,
The general cause of words, the hero's stance,
The ambitions incommensurable with flesh,
        But the drab makings of a room
Where sometimes in the afternoon of thought
                The brief and blinding flash
May light the enormous chambers of your will
And show the gracious Parthenon that time
                Is ever measured by.

As groceries in a pantry gleam and smile
        Because they are important weights
Bought with the metal minutes of your pay,
So do these hours stand in solid rows,
The dowry for a use in common life.
        I love you first because your years
Lead to my matter-of-fact and simple death
                Or to our open marriage,
And I pray nothing for my safety back,
Not even luck, because our love is whole
                Whether I live or fail.

THE VOYAGE

The ship of my body has danced in the dance of the storm
And pierced to the center the heavy embrace of the tide;
It has plunged to the bottomless trough with the knife of its
form
And leapt with the prow of its motion elate from the bride.

And now in the dawn I am salt with the taste of the wave,
Which lies with itself and suspires, her beauty asleep,
And I peer at the fishes with jaws that devour and rave
And hunt in her dream for the wrack of our hands in the
deep.

But the wind is the odor of love that awakes in the sun
The stream of our voyage that lies on the belt of the seas,
And I gather and breathe in the rays of the darkness
undone,
And drift in her silence of morning and sail at my ease,

Where the sponges and rubbery seaweeds and flowers of
hair
Uprooted abound in the water and choke in the air.

WAITRESS

Whoever with the compasses of his eyes
Is plotting the voyage of your steady shape
As you come laden through the room and back
And rounding your even bottom like a Cape
Crooks his first finger, whistles through his lip
Till you arrive, all motion, like a ship,

He is my friend—consider his dark pangs
And love of Niger, naked indigence,
Dance him the menu of a poem and squirm
Deep in the juke-box jungle, green and dense.
Surely he files his teeth, punctures his nose,
Carves out the god and takes off all his clothes.

For once, the token on the table's edge
Sufficing, proudly and with hair unpinned
You mounted the blueplate, stretched out and grinned
Like Christmas fish and turkey pink and skinned,
Eyes on the half-shell, loin with parsley stuck,
Thigh-bones and ribs and little toes to suck.

I speak to you, ports of the northern myth,
This dame is carved and eaten. One by one,
God knows what hour, her different parts go home,
Lastly her pants, and day or night is done;
But on the restaurant the sign of fear
Reddens and blazes—"English spoken here."

WASHINGTON CATHEDRAL

From summer and the wheel-shaped city
That sweats like a swamp and wrangles on
Its melting streets, white mammoth Forums,
And political hotels with awnings, caryatids;
Past barricaded embassies with trees
That shed trash and parch his eyes,
To here, the acres of superior quiet,
Shadow and damp, the tourist comes,
And, cooled by stones and darkness, stares.

Tall as a lover's night, the nave
Broods over him, irradiates,
And stars of color out of painted glass
Shoot downward on apostles and on chairs
Huddled by hundred under altar rails.
Yet it is only Thursday; there are no prayers,

But exclamations. The lady invokes by name
The thousand-odd small sculptures, spooks,
New angels, pitted roods; she gives
The inventory of relics to his heart
That aches with history and astonishment:
He gives a large coin to a wooden coffer.

Outside, noon blazes in his face like guns.
He goes down by the Bishop's walk, the dial,
The expensive grass, the Byzantine bench,
While stark behind him a red naked crane
Hangs over the unfinished transept,
A Cubist hen rivalling the Gothic School.

Whether he sees the joke; whether he cares;
Whether he tempts a vulgar miracle,
Some deus ex machina, this is his choice,
A shrine of whispers and tricky penumbras.
Therefore he votes again for the paid
Clergy, the English hint, the bones of Wilson

Crushed under tons of fake magnificence.
    Nor from the zoo of his instincts
    Come better than crude eagles: now
He cannot doubt that violent obelisk
And Lincoln whittled to a fool's colossus.
This church and city triumph in his eyes.
He is only a good alien, nominally happy.

About the Author

Karl Shapiro was born in Baltimore, Maryland, on November 10, 1913, and was educated at the University of Virginia and at Johns Hopkins University. When his first book, *Person, Place and Thing,* was published in 1942, Mr. Shapiro was already with the army in the South Pacific, where he remained until the spring of 1945. In 1946 he was appointed as Consultant in Poetry at the Library of Congress, and then, in 1947, to the faculty of Johns Hopkins University, where he taught writing courses until he resigned in 1950 to become Editor of *Poetry: A Magazine of Verse.*

The second and third of Mr. Shapiro's books—*V-Letter and Other Poems,* which was awarded the Pulitzer Prize in 1945, and *Essay on Rime*—were also published while he was on duty in the South Pacific. The fourth and most recent volume, *Trial of a Poet,* appeared in 1947.

During the years from 1940 to 1953 his poems, essays and reviews have appeared in leading literary magazines all over the world.